AGRIBUSINESS

Opportunities and Challenges

Anshul Chaudhary

ISBN-"978-81-946401-2-7"
(paperback)
First Published 2020
Publisher

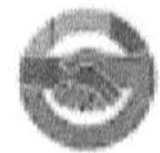

ABS Trust Publication
abstrust59@gmail.com
0172-4654022
Special Thanks to-
Editor
Siddharth Chaudhary
Head of Deptt.(RingLead, New York.)
sid@RingLead.com
+1 (267) 530-1981
Graphic Designer
Sanjiv Saini
sanjeev.ggn@gmail.com
09810548115
First Edition- 2020

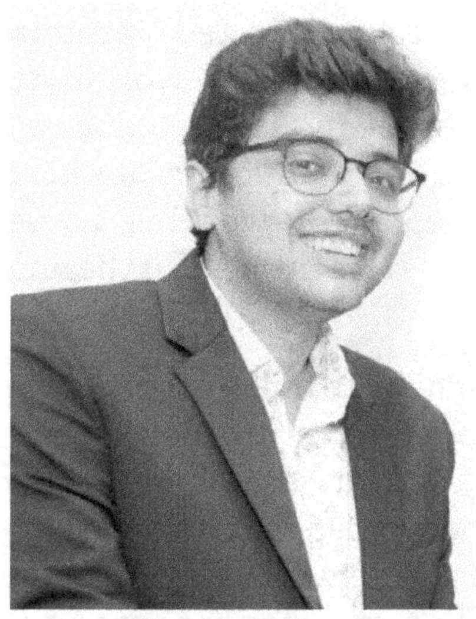

ANSHUL CHAUDHARY

(Author)
BBA(Hons) Student CHRIST, Bangalore, India
Contact- 8283871422
anshul.chaudhary@bba.christuniversity.in

PREFACE

The world is experiencing an unprecedented challenge due to COVID-19 pandemic. In the early phases of Lockdown, the most affected sector was the food and supply from producers to end consumers. The traditional supply chain was completely disrupted. Farmers were facing a dire scarcity of farm-workers to work in their fields. Harvested produce was being affected due to less developed storage facilities near production-points. Search for new and modern ways of farm-working, harvesting, storage, and transportation were the need of the hour to be devised and adopted.

In March 2020, when the university postponed the annual exams, we all have to return home. Due to Lockdown getting fresh fruits and vegetables was a real challenge. This problem encouraged me to know about more supply chains and their future which further landed me in smart farming. It was the time when the new Agriculture Reform laws were in the news. All this, being a BBA student, encouraged to write and Agribusiness was the choice!

Every day, the food we eat connects us to a vast global web of farmers, traders, food manufacturers, retailers and many other people involved in getting food from farm to fork. Most of us probably do not pause to think about it while biting into a piece of fruit or a slice of bread, but this global food system is central to some of the biggest challenges facing humanity.

I have made every effort to ensure that all data and information in this book is latest and accurate. Hereby I disclaim any liability caused by any error or omission. This is my first book, and it was indeed a huge challenge.   Hope you will appreciate my efforts as a book in your hand.

My appreciations to the elder brother, friend, and guide Siddharth Chaudhary, who helped, reinforced, and encouraged me to interpret the data and to document it. I am grateful to my family and friends for their support during my endeavour.

Anshul Chaudhary
30th November 2020
Chandigarh, India

Contents

"Business includes those human activities relating to production and distribution of goods, services and ideas with a view to earning profit."

Roger W. Babson

"To forget how to dig the earth and tend the soil is to forget ourselves."

Mahatma Gandhi

"Agribusiness is the sum of all operations involved in the manufacture and distribution of farm-supplies, production activities on farm, storage, processing and distribution of farm commodities and items made from them."

John David & Goldberg

CHAPTER-1

WHAT IS AGRIBUSINESS?

Agribusiness is associated with the business of food production, processing, and distribution industries engaged in farming. John H. Davis of Harvard University first used the term agribusiness in 1955. He defined it as "the sum of all operations involved in the production and distribution of food and fibre." In the 1980s it was used synonymously for term agriculture and agricultural economics. It includes crop production (farming or contract farming), agrichemicals, breeding, distribution, farm machinery, processing, and seed supply.

Agribusiness denotes investment in agriculture for performing any activities relating to production and distribution of agricultural products or services for making a profit. Products and services refer to both inputs and outputs of agriculture. It is one of the main generators of employment and income worldwide. It deals with the agriculture sector and also with the portion of the industrial sector.

Marketing and distribution of farm products include warehouses, wholesalers, processors, retailers, and more. Any company that participates in the production, marketing, safety, and distribution of food is involved in agribusiness.

Agribusiness usually refers to large agricultural companies in comparison with small, independent farms. However, agribusiness companies can be large or small, corporate or independent. Agribusiness is a way of describing companies and enterprises that are related to cultivating and processing food and other agricultural products

Critics of corporate farming use this term to create an aura of negativity around the concept, associating it with large corporations and companies that produce environmentally questionable, non-organic products while ensuring that smaller, potentially sustainable farms fail to turn a profit. However, the industry encompasses small- and medium-sized businesses as well as global companies.

Agribusiness encompasses items: Productive resources (feed, seed, fertiliser, equipment, energy, pesticides, machinery etc.), Agricultural commodities – (raw and processed commodities of food and fibre), Facilitative services (credit, insurance, marketing, storage, processing, transportation, packing, distribution, consultancy, soil testing etc.).
Agribusiness also includes economic activities derived from or connected to farm products. In other words, crop production, as well as crop processing, transportation and distribution. Agriculture and all of its economic, social and demographic derivatives have an impact. Financing agribusiness can increase the added value of raw materials, strengthening local rural economies, food security and nutrition, and improving the quality of life in many homes. Policies, incentives and regulatory frameworks that safeguard and promote agro-industries have proven to be highly effective at lifting rural populations out of poverty in many countries.

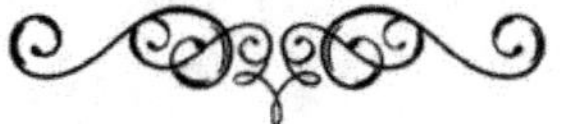

CHAPTER-2

AGRICULTURE TO AGRIBUSINESS

Why a change in approach essential?

Population growth:

According to the United Nations' projections, the world's population will reach almost 10 billion in 2050. The impact on global food systems will be substantial. Demand for food can grow 70 per cent by 2050 (compared to 2005/2007 levels). To meet this new demand, agriculture producers will need to grow almost 50 per cent more food, feed, and biofuel than they did in 2012. It means that agricultural output in South Asia will need to grow more than double by 2050 to meet increased demand. The global food system is already showing its limits in dealing with current demand. In the future, it will have to deal with population growth and increased urbanisation.
India's food security depends on producing cereal crops and increasing its production of fruits, vegetables and milk to meet the demands of a growing population.

Global warming and Climate change:
Climate change is no longer a matter of conjecture or debate. It is a fact. Climate change may be a significant dis-

ruptor in our efforts to deal with one of humankind's most significant challenges. Human activities are estimated to have caused approximately 1.0°C of global warming above pre-industrial levels. Global warming is likely to reach 1.5°C between 2030 and 2052 if it continues to increase at the current rate, according to the Intergovernmental Panel on Climate Change (IPCC) Levels of greenhouse gas (GHG) emissions are the highest in history. Climate change will affect every aspect of food production. Variability in rainfall and increases in droughts and floods are likely to reduce yields, soil quality, water-table depth, fertility, and pH all impact agricultural production.

Climate change is also likely to increase diseases' incidence, as infectious disease transmission patterns become disrupted. As such, meeting future food demand will require far-reaching reforms at every food supply chain stage.

Need for skilled people:

Modern farming demands skilled people to manage farm businesses. These people require excellent agricultural skills and competent business skills, planning skills, and good early decision-making skills. Young people entering farming with these multiple skill-sets are scarce, and this is a significant concern. The current shortage of competent farm managers with strong business skills still needs addressing. In future, many of these farm properties will require higher levels of leadership and management than those levels accepted in the past if they are to continue to grow and prosper.

Access to Information technology and data:

Gathering accurate and regular information is a real challenge for even the most competent farmers. For farmers to make accurate and reliable, early decisions industry and research organisations need to develop cost-effective and easily managed tools that can accurately assess farms and farmers performance.

Regulation and constrains:

Many farmers face current and future constraints from regulatory authorities. Issues like water quantity, good quality seeds and chemical fertilisers affect farms in the remote areas. The regulation will restrict a farmer's ability to farm to their full potential without expertise and cost. Regulatory constraints will limit future economic land-use opportunities.

Production and storage issues:

India is one of the significant cereal production countries needed to find some way for transparent supply arrangements for storage, transportation, marketing, distribution and export for its farmers to ensure the viability and continuity of farming systems. A sincere and scientific attempt is needed to mitigate all farming-related issues. Agriculture - a fundamental to the economy:

The agriculture and allied sectors are the sole bright spot amid the slide in other sectors this year of pandemic. However, the share of agriculture in the Indian economy every year has been coming down. In 2019-20, it stood at 14.7%. However, in future, it is expected to increase. The commercial and growth aspirations are important; farmers also expect their demands met in the decision process. While this is difficult when capital is scarce, the farmer's expectations add complexity to lawmakers' priorities.

These demands may consider and defend while making investment decisions.

Innovation in Agribusiness:

Innovation is a continuing endeavour among agribusinesses, as the industry seeks improved and efficient production and processing methods. For example, many companies now offer drone surveillance of farms, which gives the farmer/owner insights on crops' health and helps them create stock projections and plan for the future. New and improved machinery types are being engineered
and manufactured on a large scale, such as robotic harvesters, automated pesticide sprayers, and driverless tractors.
The aim of innovation in agribusiness is to improve agricultural productivity and make agricultural activities easier for farmers. It aims to lower the costs of production and increase profitability for farmers.

Future focus:

It is worth noting that farmers have long leveraged technological breakthroughs to adapt agricultural practices to changing times. This era is no exception, particularly with the emergence of Smart Agriculture. While there is a still enormous potential for Indian farmers to develop further, several farms are already performing at above-average production levels. The future focus for farmers should not solely be on production, but also on producing a consistently high-quality product for sale.

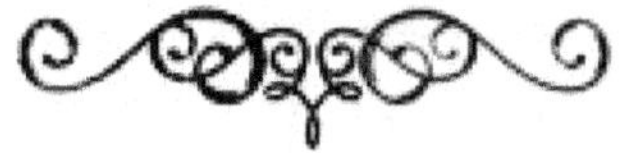

CHAPTER-3

COMPONENTS AND IMPORTANCE OF AGRIBUSINESS

Plant Breeding:

Plant breeding is the science of the improvement of plant species, through pollination, genetic engineering, and selection of progeny, to create new and improved plant genotypes and phenotypes with desirable characteristics such as disease or insect pest resistance, salt or drought tolerance, crop quality, or increased yields, etc. The Indian Agricultural Research Institute (IARI) is the country's premier national Institute for agricultural research, education and extension. The Green Revolution stemmed from the fields of IARI. Development of high yielding varieties of all major crops that occupy vast areas throughout the country, generation and standardisation of
their production, techniques, integrated pest management and integrated soil-water-nutrient management have been the Institute's hallmarks research.

Agrichemicals:

Agrichemicals or agrochemicals are the pesticides, fertilisers, and growth chemicals used in the agricultural process. Today, many agrochemical companies, such as UPL Ltd, BASF India Ltd, P I Industries Ltd, Bayer Crop Science Ltd etc. work to supply the agriculture industry with chemicals and other innovative solutions.

Machinery and Equipment:

The machinery and equipment segment of agribusiness is one of the biggest, and it refers to all types of farm machinery – ranging from hand tools, such as shovels, to tractors. One of the largest agricultural machinery companies is John Deere, specialising in providing farming and gardening equipment. Over the years, the Mahindra Tractors has emerged as one of the top manufacturers of agricultural and farm equipment, including tractors in India.

Importance of Agribusiness:

Agriculture is the economic sector that employs the most people in the world and the primary source of food and income for many people living in poverty. Thus, investing in agriculture is not only one of the most effective strategies to improve food security and promote sustainability; it is also essential to many countries'
economic development.
Therefore, we can say that agribusiness supports the growth of the agricultural industry, which is pivotal to economic growth. It also continues to play a crucial role in the growth of developing countries. Agribusinesses can potentially improve agricultural productivity, which is why governments often offer subsidies to agricultural businesses.

Agricultural activities also contribute to an improved food security system and sustainable food production and income for a majority of the poor in developing countries. According to the Food and Agriculture Organization of the

United Nations (FAO), over 70 per cent of the world's food needs a met by small farmers only.

Global Competitiveness of Indian Agribusiness:

Indian agribusiness is being seen as an essential arena for creating employment and income for large sections of India's rural and agrarian population in the coming years and decades by public agencies, nationally and globally. It is happening in the context of vital agribusiness sectors in China's neighbouring countries and those in the South-East and East Asia. In the global context of agribusiness competitiveness from an Indian perspective, we have to focus on the global trade regime and few critical sectors like cereals, fruits and vegetables and identify major factors in their export performance from a value chain perspective. We should also look at critical global trade policies at the World Trade Organisation (WTO).

Attributes of successful agribusiness:

 Good leadership and support, good planning, critical decision-making, and hard work can achieve any business's goals and objectives. Critical decision processes include gathering good information and discussion between farm managers and scientific advisors. For any business, success is born out of higher longer-term profitability. Changes in operational management and changes in governance focus can reduce the input cost of seeds and fertilisers. There has been structured investment in product development, infrastructure and farm systems to make these businesses as resilient as possible.
Overview

So, agribusiness is a term used to describe the sector that

encompasses all economic activities related to farming, i.e., chemicals, breeding, crop production/farming, farm machinery, distribution, marketing, and sales.

Examples of agribusiness include farm machinery manufacturing, seed supply, and agrichemicals. Agribusiness companies produce, market, and distribute agricultural products and supports. Some agribusiness companies manufacture farming equipment, agrichemicals, or other farm products.

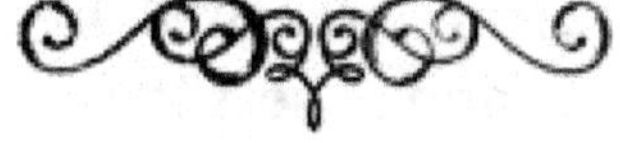

CHAPTER-4

MAJOR AGRICULTURAL PROBLEMS OF INDIA AND THEIR POSSIBLE SOLUTIONS

Indian agriculture is troubled by several problems; some are natural, and others are manmade.

Small and fragmented land-holdings:

India's total geographical area is 329 million hectares. The seeming abundance of net sown area of 141.2 million hectares and total cropped area of 189.7 million hectares (1999-2000) pales into insignificance due to economically unviable small and scattered holdings. Agriculture Census, the average size of operational holdings has decreased from 2.28 hectares in 1970-71 to 1.84 hectares in 1980-81, to 1.41 hectares in 1995-96 and 1.08 hectares in 2015-16. Considering declining trends, observed in the
size of landholdings, in the past and the future increase in population over time, the fragmentation of holdings is likely to continue. The average size of operational holdings may further decrease.

Small and fragmented holdings are more severe in densely populated and intensively cultivated states like Kerala, West Bengal, Bihar and Uttar Pradesh. The average size of land holdings is less than one hectare. Rajasthan with vast sandy stretches and Nagaland with the prevailing 'Jhoom' (shifting agriculture) have larger average-sized holdings of 4 and 7.15 hectares. States with a high percentage of a net sown area like Punjab, Haryana, Maharashtra, Gujarat, Karnataka and Madhya Pradesh hold size above the national average.

It is important to note that a large proportion of 59% holdings in 1990-91 were marginal (below 1 hectare) accounting for 14.9 per cent of the total operated area. Another 19 % were smallholdings (1-2 hectare) taking up 17.3 per cent of the total operated area. Large holdings (above 10 hectares) accounted for only 1.6% per cent of total holdings but covered 17.4 per cent of the operated area. Hence, there is a wide gap between small farmers, medium farmers (peasant group) and big farmers (landlords).

As per inheritance laws, the land belonging to the father is equally divided among his children. In this way, the holdings become smaller and more fragmented with each passing generation. It is one of the main causes of our low agricultural productivity and our agriculture's backward state. A lot of time and labour is wasted in moving seeds, manure and implements from one small field to another. Irrigation becomes difficult on such small and fragmented fields. Further, much fertile agricultural land wasted in providing boundaries.

The only answer to this ticklish problem is the consolidation of holdings. The other solution to this problem is cooperative farming in which the farmers pool their resources and share the profit.

Expensive high-quality Seeds:

The seed is a critical and basic input for attaining higher crop yields. Distribution of assured quality seed is as critical as the production of such seeds. Unfortunately, good quality seeds are out of reach for most farmers, especially small and marginal farmers, mainly because of higher prices. In order to solve this problem, the Government of India established the National Seeds Corporation (NSC) in 1963, the State Farmers Corporation of India (SFCI) in 1969 and a thirteen State Seed Corporations (SSCs) to boost the supply of High Yielding Variety Programme (HYVP) to the farmers. These corporations have to move a step forward and supply cheaper hybrids to farmers.

Farmers should be encouraged to use the certified seed of improved varieties in order to increase national production. Adequate incentives could be provided to seed producers to supply seed in sufficient quantity to meet demand—subsidies given as a part of a government policy of assistance to farmers for specific crops. In Turkey, subsidies are part of transitional arrangements to encourage the private sector to enter the seed-market. Turkey government arranged for subsidies paid to private companies. Small loans disbursed at nominal interest to small farmers for growing exotic and hybrid verities.
Supply of Manures, Fertilisers and Biocides:

Indian soils have been used for growing crops over thousands of years without caring much for replenishing. It has led to depletion and exhaustion of soils resulting in their low productivity. The average yields of almost all the crops are among the lowest in the world. It is a serious problem solved by using more manures and fertilisers. Chemical fertilisers are costly and are often beyond the reach of the poor farmers. The fertiliser problem is, therefore, both acute and complex.

The government has given high subsidy for using chemical fertilisers. As a result of the government's initiative and due to change in some progressive farmers' attitude, fertilisers' consumption increased tremendously.

To maintain the quality of the fertilisers, 52 fertiliser quality control laboratories have been set up in different parts of the country. There are one Central Fertilizer Quality Control and Training Institute at Faridabad with its three regional centres at Mumbai, Kolkata and Chennai.

Biocides (pesticides, herbicides and weedicides) used to save the crops and to avoid losses. The increased use of these inputs has saved many crops, especially the food crops, from unnecessary wastage. However, indiscriminate use of biocides has resulted in widespread environmental pollution, which takes its toll.

It felt that organic manures are essential for keeping the soil in good health. The country has a potential of 650 million tonnes of rural and 160 lakh tonnes of urban compost which not fully utilised. The utilisation of this potential will solve the twin problem of disposal of waste and providing manure to the soil.

Irrigation:

Although India is the second-largest irrigated country in the world after China, only one-third of the cropped area is under irrigation. Irrigation is the most important agricultural input in a tropical monsoon country like India where rainfall is uncertain, unreliable and erratic. India cannot achieve sustained progress in agriculture unless more than half of the cropped area brought under assured irrigation. The monsoon has often been called the real finance minister due to agriculture's dependence on it. On the other hand, due to over and intensive irrigation, especially in areas irrigated by canals like in Punjab and Haryana large areas are rendered useless (areas affected by salinity, alkalinity and water-logging).

Improved irrigation is the key to agriculture. Expansion of irrigation coverage via efficient micro-irrigation technologies, the cultivation of less water-intensive crops, and a revamp of research and extension services are needed to utilise water efficiently. The modern irrigation methods, including sprinkler systems, drip systems, etc., are also used in some parts of the country to overcome this problem.

Lack of mechanisation:

Despite the large scale mechanisation of agriculture, most agricultural operations are carried out manually using conventional tools in remote areas of the country, especially by small and marginal farmers. It results in huge wastage of human labour and low yields per capita labour force. There is an urgent need to mechanise the agricultural operations to avoid wastage of labour force and make farming convenient and efficient.

Strenuous efforts made to encourage the farmers to own tractors, power tillers, combine harvesters, irrigation pumps and other technically advanced agricultural equipment for efficient and timely agricultural operations. It will help in facilitating multiple cropping and economise the agricultural production process.

Degrading soil quality and Soil erosion:

Soil degradation is the loss of the intrinsic physical, chemical, or biological qualities of soil either by natural or human activities. The main causes of soil degradation are soil erosion, organic matter decline and unsustainable agricultural practices. Soil degradation directly results in the loss of land's production capacity due to loss of soil fertility.

This land requires treatment and restoration to its original fertility. To manage soil fertility of these farms, more efficiently in future soil testing becomes essential. Addition of manure/organic fertilisers advised and promoted to use as per the crops' needs to be grown in that field. Scientific methods must be financed at local levels to convert agricultural waste into farm manure. It will reduce the cost of farm input and increase soil fertility in an eco-friendly way.

Agricultural Marketing:

There is a deep segmentation of agricultural markets in India, and farm incomes will boost. The Rural Credit Survey Report rightly remarked that the producers, in general, sell their produce at an unfavourable place, at an unfavourable time and get unfavourable terms. Farmers sometimes even cheated by the use of false weights and are charged a high commission.

An announcement in 2018 aimed towards providing farmers with better sales infrastructure was the promise to convert village markets into agricultural markets. In 2018, the Centre said it would convert 22,000 such village markets into agricultural markets. However, not a single such village market has is converted into an agricultural market.

New Agri-laws are paving the ways for private markets but not providing enough safeguards to stop farmers' exploitation. Time-tested schemes like the minimum support price subsidy (MSP) and government procurement at APMC mandis help farmers sell their products better. Further reforms in the Agricultural Market must be focused to safeguard interests and future of small and marginal farmers.

Price crash and inadequate storage facilities:

The Indian farmer today faces a peculiar challenge. If his crop is bad, due to natural calamity or spurious seed or pesticide, there may be a rise in prices. Since this results in food inflation and attracts the media's attention, the government comes in with a heavy hand in action under the Essential Commodities Act. It then depresses the prices, and the farmer bears the brunt. It was the case of onion in November and December 2019.

If nature is benevolent and the crop is good, production may turn out to be more than what domestic demand requires. In this case, the farmer also suffers because prices crash, and sometimes the farmer cannot recover even his cultivation cost. An example was the onion in Kharif 2017 when Madhya Pradesh's onion prices crashed to Rs 200 per quintal. So, if crops' productivity goes up substantially, the domestic market may not absorb the same, and the prices will fall steeply.

Storage facilities in rural areas are either totally absent or grossly inadequate. Under such conditions, the farmers compelled to sell their produce immediately after the harvest at the prevailing market prices which are bound to be low. Such distress sale deprives the farmers of their legitimate income.

If farmers had access to appropriate and affordable storage facilities, it would enable them to store and make sales in a staggered manner throughout the year. It would also mean that consumers, on the other hand, do not have to face a sudden rise in the price of onions, for example, in the off-season.

The 'operation Green' (in 2018) was supposed to create new and better storage facilities, facilitate food processing industries and compress supply chains to aid farmers. It was supposed to assist in realising a better price for the consumers and better equipped to deal with the market's whims.

The Parse Committee estimated the post-harvest losses at 9.3 per cent of which nearly 6.6 per cent occurred due to poor storage conditions alone. Scientific storage is, therefore, very essential to avoid losses and to benefit the farmers and the consumers alike. At present, there are several agencies engaged in warehousing and storage activities. The Food Corporation of India (F.C.I.), the Central Warehousing Corporation (C.W.C.) and State Warehousing Corporation are among the principal agencies engaged in this task. National Grid of Rural Godowns initiated during 1979-80 needs revolutionisation. This scheme will provide storage facilities to the farmers near their fields and small and marginal farmers.

Inadequate transport:

One of the main handicaps with Indian agriculture is the lack of cheap and efficient means of transportation. Even at present, there are lakhs of villages still not well-connected with market centres. Linking each village by metalled road is a gigantic task, and it needs huge sums of money to complete this task.

Economic Issues -Scarcity of capital:

Agriculture is an important industry, and like all other industries, it also requires capital. The role of capital input is becoming more and more important with the advancement of farm technology. The main suppliers of money to the farmer are the money-lenders, traders and commission agents who charge a high-interest rate. All India Rural Credit Survey Committee showed that Central Cooperative Banks, State Cooperative Banks, Commercial Banks, Cooperative Credit Agencies and some Government Agencies extend loans to farmers easily.

Insurance of crops gives security from adverse situations. In this direction, Pradhan Mantri Fasal Bima Yojana launched in January 2016. Crucially, it allowed private players entry into the crop insurance market. All farmers who availed of credit on their Kisan Credit Cards (KCC) compulsorily enrolled in the scheme. A subsidised amount of insurance premium deducted from their loan amounts. The key problem with this scheme delayed settlement of claims. The timeliness of settlement of a claim is crucial because farmers are short on working capital to sow for the next crop after suffering crop loss. Insurance claim settlement can bridge that gap if provided quickly enough.

Linking MGNREGA to agriculture could provide a way for the government to pay as a part of agricultural wages. PM Kisan scheme is by far the best performing agricultural scheme and 11 crore farmers benefitted with Rs. 6000 per year.

Climate Change: The Great Disruptor

Climate change is a real fact now and affecting every aspect of food production. Variability in rainfall and increases in droughts and floods are likely to reduce yields, soil quality, water-table depth, fertility, and pH all impact agricultural production. Climate change is also likely to increase diseases' incidence, as infectious disease transmission patterns become disrupted.

Need for new policies:

How modern farming businesses will operate is not easily understood by many of the elected representatives. Many of them disconnected from their rural roots. Indian agriculture is a victim of past successes, especially the green revolution, and needs a paradigm shift in policies and priorities for a structural makeover.

A favourable minimum support price (MSP) for growing less water-intensive crops like pulses and oilseeds is essential and must back by a strong procurement system. Maise

takes less water and has a large domestic and global market. If facilities for drying maise in mandis provided to farmers, they can get a fair price.

New agri-laws, reforms or policies are needed to favour agribusiness after due discussion and all stakeholders' participation to meet future demands. The farmers will require essential support and subsidies to set the pace for the third green revolution.

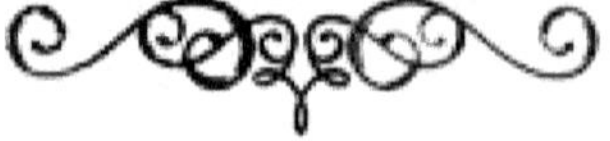

CHAPTER-5

MARKET REFORMS

Indian agriculture is harnessing the emerging global opportunities. Three high-level committees, the Hooda Committee, the Swaminathan Committee, and the Shanta Kumar Committee, recommended market reforms after a wide range of consultations with many stakeholders, including farmers and farmer associations. The reform measures expected to tap the potential of agro-processing and export of agricultural commodities. It includes farmers' access to improved technologies and good management practices, even as prices and procurement are assured. These will increase farmers' incomes and generate new employment opportunities, especially in logistics, packaging, transport, processing, etc. However, the success of reforms will create an enabling business environment, especially for e-retailing, organised retailing, agro-processing and exports.

During the Covid-19 pandemic, special packages have been announced for the farm sector to develop infrastructure, promote diversification, and strengthen MSMEs in the agro-processing sector. The export of agricultural commodities has also given emphasis. To attract agri-business, various provisions made through institutional arrangements for harnessing economies-of-scale through FPOs, contract farming, cluster farming, 'one district, one product', SHGs, etc. All these measures are to create an enabling agri-business environment for inclusive, efficient and sustainable agriculture.

Agricultural marketing plays an important role in stimulating production and consumption and accelerating the pace of economic development. It is the most important multiplier of agricultural development. Availability of a transparent, easily accessible, and efficient marketing platform is a prerequisite to ensure farmers' remunerative prices.

How has the agri-marketing policy changed over the years?

1. In 2016, the Electronic National Agricultural Market (E-NAM) launched. The e-NAM intended to be a market-based mechanism for efficient price discovery by the farmers. In the first phase, 585 markets across 16 States and 2 Union Territories covered. States needed to amend their respective Agricultural Produce Market Committee (APMC) Acts to put in place three prerequisites for the success of this programme —
   - A single licence across the State;
   - A single-point levy of the market fee;
   - Electronic auctioning in all the markets

Reason for failure of e-Nam: The several States could not or did not carry out these amendments, and the e-NAM proved to be far less effective than desired.

2. In September 2018, the government launched PM-AASHA- to provide an assured price to

farmers that ensured a return of at least 50% more than the cost of cultivation. The programme was confined to pulses and oilseeds to limit the fiscal costs. However, many other crops, which did not receive the MSP-procurement system's benefits, also needed this coverage. Public procurement, deficiency payments and private procurement were the main planks of this programme

Reason for the uninspiring performance of PM-AASHA

Only public procurement carried out in a meaningful way. Deficiency payments only implemented on a pilot basis in Madhya Pradesh. Private procurement was not initiated, even on a pilot basis, in any State. The budgetary allocation was meagre: only ₹500 crores earmarked in 2020-2021.

3. Late Arun Jaitley announced TOP (tomatoes, onions and potatoes) scheme to stabilise these farm products' prices through processing and storage. He also allocated Rs 500 crore for it. The scheme entrusted to the Ministry of Food

4. Processing for implementation. However, even after three years of the scheme, not even 5 per cent of the money promised has been spent. No wonder, the government is back to export bans of onions, fearing a spike in onion prices. It seems the government has one foot on the accelerator to liberalise Agri markets, and the other foot is on the brake (ban on onion exports).

5. In 2019, PM-KISAN Yojana- This programme involved a fixed payment of ₹6,000 per annum to

each farm household with a budgetary outlay of ₹75,000 crores. This programme has worked reasonably well so far with many States topping up the amount at their end.

Agriculture Produce Marketing Committee (APMC)

Agricultural markets in India mainly regulated by state Agriculture Produce Marketing Committee (APMC) laws. APMCs ensure fair trade between buyers and sellers for effective price discovery of farmers' produce. APMCs can regulate the trade of farmers' produce by providing licenses to buyers, commission agents, and private markets, levy market fees or any other charges on such trade, and provide necessary infrastructure within their markets to facilitate the trade.

Drawbacks of APMCs-

APMC laws are not implemented in their true sense and need to reform urgently. Most APMCs have a limited number of traders operating, which leads to cartelisation

and reduces competition. Undue deductions in the form of commission charges (from the buyer and seller) and market fees (0.5% to 5%) are taken. Traders, commission agents, and other functionaries organise themselves into associations (delayed elections), which do not allow easy entry of new persons into market yards, stifling competition. Thus, APMC markets have become monopsonistic (too many sellers and one buyer) with high commission costs. Further mandi fees on inter-state trade amount to double taxation, besides violating the idea of a single national market. The Acts are highly restrictive in promoting multiple marketing channels (such as more buyers, private markets, direct sale to businesses and retail consumers, and online transactions) and competition.

Moreover, APMC mandis cater only to only 1/3rd of total marketed farm produce with the rest of the products sold outside these mandis

The central government passed three Acts together in September 2020 to increase farmers' opportunities to enter long term sale contracts, increase the availability of buyers, and permit buyers to purchase farm produce in bulk. The passing of the farm bills has sparked a major controversy in the country.

1. The Farmers' Produce Trade and Commerce (Promotion and Facilitation) Act, 2020: The act allows intra-state and inter-state trade of farmers' produce outside the physical premises of market yards run by market committees formed under the

2. State APMC Acts. Electronic trading and transaction platforms facilitate the direct and online buying and selling of such products by the companies, partnership firms, registered societies, a farmer producer organisation or agricultural cooperative society. Market fee abolished.

3. The Farmers (Empowerment and Protection) Agreement on Price Assurance and Farm Services Bill, 2020: The act allows Farming agreement between a farmer and a buyer before producing or rearing any farm produce. The price of farming produce should mention in the agreement. It provides for a three-level dispute settlement mechanism: the conciliation

> board, Sub-Divisional Magistrate and Appellate Authority.

4. **The Essential Commodities (Amendment) act, 2020:** The act provides that the central government regulate the supply of certain food items including cereals, pulses, potatoes, onions, edible oilseeds, and oils, only under extraordinary circumstances. These include war, famine, extraordinary price rise and, a natural calamity of grave nature. The imposition of any stock limit on agricultural produce based on price rise.

Effects of new farm laws on Present system of APMC:

Acts introduced to effectively bypass the Agricultural Produce Market Committee (APMC) markets. There is no doubt that several problems have marred APMC markets. However, it does not mean that APMC markets are inherently problematic.

APMC markets are the "last resort for millions of marginal and small farmers who would never be attractive to corporate buyers, individually or perhaps even collectively, through FPOs."

For instance, the repeal of the APMC Act in Bihar back in 2006 ostensibly for enabling free private trade in agriculture has not helped the farmers in the state. They have to sell their produce year after year well below the MSP. It has not ensured private investment in the development of market yards. Therefore, the need has been to reform the existing APMC markets and sub-markets in the rural areas and create newer ones to reduce the burden on the existing ones.

Small farmers, especially marginalised castes and communities are less literate and generally excluded from modern market arrangements, like contract farming or direct purchase.

Further, once the farmer takes farm produce to the mandi, he cannot bring it back as it is like taking a dead body to the mortuary. It is here that the role of the market becomes crucial as even if a farmer has produced efficiently but is not able to sell well, the story is lost. Therefore, the distress among small farmers in India is market-driven to a large extent in both ways-too much protection (MSP) or too little protection. Whatever new market channels like contract farming and direct purchase may emerge for farmers, small farmers will continue to depend on APMC markets for many commodities.

Therefore, it is important to ensure the fair functioning of such markets. In terms of the open auction, proper unloading and storage/handling of farmer produce, especially perishable, is essential. Later is generally auctioned from the roadside and filthy grounds and stopping commission charged to farmer sellers even in some states' regulated markets.

APMC markets also serve as the main competitors to contract farming and direct purchase, and they discover their prices based on APMC prices. Therefore, their better functioning can improve the terms offered to contract growers and direct sellers. Warehouse receipts system needs to be extended all crops with the facility's expansion to free farmers from credit and output linkage and avoid distress sale immediately after harvest.

Therefore, solutions go beyond produce markets, whereas

recent reforms are more about regulatory changes that do not concern most Indian farmers as they do not have access to APMC markets. Small farmers need to collectivise into groups and FPOs, including Farmer Producer Companies (both pre-production and post-production) to lower transaction cost for private buyers and gain some bargaining power in the new markets.

The government must allow states to decide about APMCs and contract farming. States should be authorised to make their laws about the functioning of APMCs, cess and development of mandis. The Centre can provide a framework of guiding principles by making a Model Marketing Act.
Small rural markets can emerge as a viable alternative for agricultural marketing if provided with adequate infrastructure facilities.

Gramin Agricultural Markets scheme (which aims to improve infrastructure and civic facilities in 22,000 Gramin Haats across the country) should be made a fully funded central scheme and scaled to ensure a Haat's presence in each panchayat of the country.
Prices determined by the nature of the commodity, demand, supply and global prices, and therefore, it is impossible to have legally-guaranteed prices. Here are a few other 'concerns': that the corporate sector will exploit smallholders and acquire their lands, that the dispute settlement mechanism is cumbersome, etc.

MSP made legal, implying that all private players buying below this price would be fined or jailed. That may spell disaster in the markets, and private players will shun buying. Moreover, the Government can ensure farmers that it will continue to buy farm produce for Public Distribution System (PDS) and buffer stock only from farmers at MSP and never from private players.

The new farm laws will help India emerge as a leader in agriculture and agro-processing. They expect to build a new crop of agri-tech start-ups and innovation hubs in the farm sector. Public representatives, from sarpanch to the MP/MLA should meet farmers and farmer organisations in their areas to be well informed about these laws. The government must not hesitate to amend the laws to favour the farmers at large.

New laws provide greater choice and freedom to farmers to sell their produce, to the companies to buy and store, creating competition in agricultural marketing. This competition expects to help build more efficient value chains in agriculture by reducing marketing costs, enabling better price discovery, improving price realisation for farmers and, at the same time, reducing the price paid by consumers.

It will also encourage private investment in storage, thus reducing wastage and containing seasonal price volatility. Good ideas/laws should not fail because of bad implementation. Coordination between the Central & State governments, and also among various States becomes crucial for the success of any policy reforms.

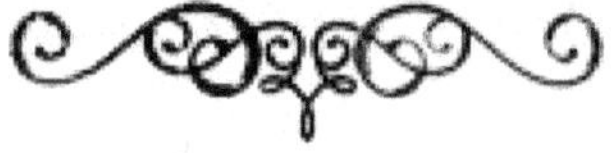

CHAPTER-6

AGRIBUSINESS IDEAS WITH LOW CAPITAL INVESTMENT

Agriculture is one of the most growing and demanding sectors in today's era. There are more than 100 agriculture businesses that are growing these days rapidly. Some of these agriculture businesses can be done in less capital, while some may require huge capital investment.

The agriculture sector is a very large and vast sector that includes many other things like forestry, animal husbandry, and fisheries. If the agriculture-related business, done with passion and commitment, one can earn a very good income.

To start an agribusiness, two things are essential –one's ability to work and how much one can one invest in that business.

Dairy business:

The demand for milk, as well as milk products always remains high. Hence we can say that the dairy business is the most profitable agribusiness in India.

Mushroom farming:

The business of mushroom farming can give more profit in less time—moreover; it is done at less expense and less space. The demand for mushroom has increased these days in hotels, restaurants as well as homes.

Production of organic manure:

These days preparing vermicompost and organic fertiliser are becoming a domestic business. This business is done in low capital investment along with little awareness of its production process.

Fertiliser Distribution Business:

This business can be done easily by people living in small cities or rural areas. In the fertiliser distribution business, one has to buy fertilisers from big cities and sell them to rural areas.

Dry flower business:

In the past ten years, there has been a great increase in the trade of dried flowers. Farmers can cultivate flowers in small fields, dry them and sell to craft stores or those who are fond of flowers.

Tree Farming:

If someone has large lands but less time for farming can earn profits by growing and selling trees. It takes a long time till the trees grow, due to which this business takes time to give profits. However, it comes under the category of good and profitable agriculture business.

Hydroponic Retail Store:

The use of hydroponics technology is increasing very fast these days. In a hydroponics system, plants/crops cultivated without soil. In this business, one can sell much hydroponics equipment in one place.

Organic Greenhouse:

The growth of the organic greenhouse business is also very good because the demand for organically grown products is increasing, and people are now buying land to build organic greenhouses.

Tea leaf plantations:

Due to the increasing demand for tea leaves, a person can earn good profit through this business. However, for growing tea leaves, the choice of weather and place is very important. Though capital investment in this business is high, but in return, profit is also high.

Beekeeping:

As many people today have become health-conscious, the demand for honey is also increasing. Thus a trained beekeeper farmer and growing flowers and medicinal plants can earn a good profit from the same fields without any extra cost.

Export of fruits and vegetables:

All you need to do is buy fruits and vegetables from local farms or farmers and supply them to big cities or urban areas using scientific methods of packaging, storage and transportation. Export of fruits and vegetables is a very profitable business with low investment.

Cultivation of Medicinal Herbs:

Cultivation of medicinal plants and herbs is yet another profitable agriculture business. If someone has a basic knowledge of medicinal plants and has enough land, they can earn good profits from its cultivation. At the same time, the government also offers subsidies for cultivating medicinal plants.

Maize farming:

Corn or maize has emerged as the most versatile crop. It can be grown under different climatic conditions with less water usage. By selecting good-quality maize seeds, one will get bumper yield with lower input cost and using modern drier machines; more profits earned.

Spices Processing:

Demand for organic spices is all over the world. We need spices at home also. Its processing and packaging process is not very difficult and can start with less capital investment.

Potato Powder Business;

Potato powder is used extensively in the snack food industry. It is used in all types of dishes that require mashed potatoes. Moreover, in making vegetable gravy and soup. Hence one can think of starting this business.

Cultivation of Vegetables:

If you have cultivable land and people who can work on it, start growing different local and exotic vegetables. Good quality and high yields can lead to good profits.

Soybean Cultivation:

Many types of food items like soy milk, soy flour, soy

sauce, soybean oil, etc., are prepared from soybean. If you have vacant land, then you can earn a profit by cultivating soybean in it.

Certified seed dealer:

You can also start selling good quality or certified seeds. In order to do this business, some procedures completed. There is no need to invest much capital in it.

Production of Potato Chips:

The demand for French fries and potato chips is constantly increasing worldwide; hence you can think of starting a potato chip business. It is a very profitable business with low capital investment.

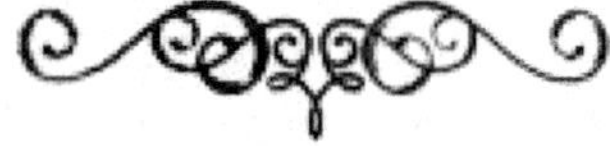

CHAPTER-7

SMART FARMING

Smart Farming is an emerging concept that refers to managing farms using modern Information and Communication Technologies to increase the quantity and quality of products while optimising human labour requirements.

Smart farming focuses on providing the agricultural industry with the infrastructure to leverage advanced technology – including big data, the cloud and the internet of things (IoT) – for tracking, monitoring, automating and analysing operations.

Smart farming is software-managed and sensor-monitored. It is growing in importance due to the combination of the expanding global population, the increasing demand for higher crop yield, the need to use natural resources

efficiently, the rising use and sophistication of information & communication technology and the increasing need for climate-smart agriculture.

Smart Farming focuses on using data acquired through various sources (historical, geographical and instrumental) in the management of farm activities. Smart farming's driving force is IoT—connecting smart machines and sensors integrated on farms to make farming processes data-driven and data-enabled. Armed with such tools, farmers can monitor field conditions without even going to the fields and making strategic decisions for the whole farm or a single plant.

We should remember that any technologically advanced system does not essentially mean that it is a smart system. Smart systems differentiate themselves through their ability to record the data and make sense out of it.

Smart farming employs hardware (IoT) and software (SaaS) to capture the data and give actionable insights to manage all the farm operations, both pre and post-harvest. Organized Data is accessible all the time and can be accessed from anywhere in the world.

Among the technologies available for present-day farmers are:

1. Sensors: soil, water, light, humidity, temperature management
2. Software: specialised software solutions that target specific farm types or use case agnostic

   IoT platforms
3. Connectivity: cellular, LoRa technology, etc.
4. Location: GPS, Satellite, etc.
5. Robotics: Autonomous tractors, processing facilities, etc.
6. Data analytics: standalone analytics solutions, data pipelines for downstream solutions, et

Differences between traditional and smart farming:

Traditional farming:

- The same set of practices for cultivation of a crop throughout the region
- Manual maintenance of all the field and collecting data leading to errors
- Application of fertilisers and pesticides throughout the field
- Geo-tagging and zone detection not possible
- No way to predict the weather

Smart farming:

- Each farm is analysed to see the suitable crops and water requirements for optimisation. Farmers can schedule and apply the right amount of water to crops, reducing waste and costs.
- Early detection and application of pesticides at the infected/affected region only, saving costs
- Field and finance data available in the same place showing the profits, yields and patterns with simple reports.
- Farmers can oversee storage conditions; receive alerts and better track and quality control of the entire supply chain.
- Satellite imagery detects the different zones in farms
- Weather analysis and prediction
- Farmers can monitor soil quality from the surface to roots, compare areas, modulate fertilising, analyse historical patterns and better manage crops long-term.

Smart Farming: The Future of Agriculture

"Smart farming" is an emerging concept that refers to managing farms using technologies like IoT, robotics, drones and AI to increase the quantity and quality of products while optimising the human labour required by production. The Internet of Things (IoT) has provided not only a way to better measure and control growth factors, like irrigation and fertiliser, on a farm, it will also change how we view agriculture in its entirely.

How automation and robotics help?

IoT (Internet of Things) in agriculture involves sensors, drones and robots connected through the internet, which function automatically and semi-automatically performing operations and gathering data to increase efficiency and predictability.

Due to the increase in demands and labour shortage across the globe, agriculture automation and robots, commonly known as Agribots, are gaining attention among farmers. Recent advancements in sensors and AI technology are helping in agrobotics revolution. However, most of the products are still in trial phases and R&D mode.

Semi-automatic robots with arms can detect weeds and spray pesticides in the affected plants, save up the plants and overall pesticide costs—these robots used in harvesting and lifting. Heavy farming vehicles can also be navigated from the comfort of homes through phone screens to perform tasks, and GPS can track their positions at every time.

Drones equipped with sensors and cameras are used for imaging, mapping and surveying the farms. They can be remotely controlled, or they can fly automatically through software-controlled flight plans in their embedded systems, working in coordination with sensors and GPS. From the drone data, insights drawn regarding crop health, irrigation, spraying, planting, soil and field, plant counting and yield prediction and much more.

IoT Solutions to Agricultural Problems:

Precision farming:

IoT can add value to all areas of farming, from growing crops to forestry. Precision farming is one of the major areas of agriculture that IoT can revolutionise. Precision farming/ agriculture is an umbrella concept for IoT-based approaches that make farming more controlled and accurate. In simple words, plants get precisely the treatment they need, determined by machines with superhuman accuracy. The biggest difference from the classical approach is that precision farming allows decisions to be made per square meter or even per plant rather than for a field.

By precisely measuring variations within a field, farmers can boost the effectiveness of pesticides and fertilisers, or use them selectively.

Developing Management Information Systems:

Planned systems for collecting, processing, storing, and disseminating data in the form is needed to carry out a farm's operations and functions.

Agricultural automation and robotics:

It is the process of applying robotics, automatic control and artificial intelligence techniques at all levels of agricultural production, including farm robots and farm drones.

Automation in Smart Greenhouses:

Traditional greenhouses control the environmental parameters through manual intervention or a proportional control mechanism, resulting in production loss, energy loss, and increased labour cost.

IoT-driven smart greenhouses can intelligently monitor and control the climate, eliminating the need for manual intervention. Various sensors deployed to measure the environmental parameters according to the specific requirements of the crop—that data stored in a cloud-based platform for further processing and control with minimal manual intervention.

Agricultural Drones:

Agriculture can incorporate both ground-based and aerial drones for crop health assessment, irrigation, crop monitoring, crop spraying, planting, soil and field analysis and other spheres.

Since drones collect multispectral, thermal and visual imagery while flying, the data they gather provide farmers with insights into a whole array of metrics: plant health indices, plant counting and yield prediction, plant height measurement, canopy cover mapping, field water pond mapping, scouting reports, stockpile measuring, chlorophyll measurement, nitrogen content in wheat, drainage mapping, weed pressure mapping, and so on.

IoT-based smart farming targets large-scale farming operations. It can add value to emerging trends in agriculture like organic farming, family farming, including breeding particular cattle or growing specific cultures, preserving particular or high-quality varieties etc., and enhancing highly transparent farming to consumers, society and market consciousness.

Internet of Food, or Farm 2020:

If we have the Internet of Things (IoT) and the Internet of Medical Things (IoMT), why not have one for food? The European Commission project Internet of Food and Farm 2020 (IoF2020), a part of Horizon 2020 Industrial

Leadership explores the potential of IoT technologies for the European food and farming industry through research and regular conferences. IoT has fostered the belief that a smart network of sensors, actuators, cameras, robots, drones, and other connected devices will bring an unprecedented level of control and automated decision-making to agriculture, making possible an enduring ecosystem of innovation in this eldest of industries.

Third Green Revolution:

Smart Farming and IoT-driven agriculture are paving the way for what can be called a Third Green Revolution.

Following the plant breeding and genetics revolutions, the Third Green Revolution is taking over agriculture. That revolution draws upon the combined application of data-driven analytics technologies, such as precision farming equipment, IoT, "big data" analytics, Unmanned Aerial Vehicles (UAVs or drones), robotics, etc.

In the future, the smart farming revolution will decrease the use of pesticide and fertiliser, while overall efficiency will rise. IoT technologies will enable better food traceability, which in turn will lead to increased food safety. It will also be beneficial for the environment, for example, more efficient use of water and farm inputs.

Therefore, smart farming has a real potential to deliver a more productive and sustainable form of agricultural production. From the farmer's point of view, Smart Farming should provide the farmer with added value in better decision-making and more efficient exploitation of operations and management.

Smart farming technologies:

The intelligent farm includes the use of technology such as:

- Sensors for soil scanning and water, light, humidity and temperature management
- Telecommunications technologies such as advanced networking and GPS
- Hardware and software for specialised applications and for enabling IoT-based solutions, robotics and automation
- Data analytics tools for decision making and prediction: Data collection is a significant part of smart farming as the quantity of data available from crop yields, soil-mapping, climate change, fertiliser applications, weather data, machinery and animal health continues to escalate.
- Satellites and drones for gathering data around the clock for an entire field: This information is forwarded to IT systems for tracking and analysis to give an "eye in the field" or "eye in the barn" that makes remote monitoring possible.
- Combining these technologies facilitates machine-to-machine (M2M) derived data: This

data feeds into a decision support system so that farmers can see what is happening at a more granular level than in the past. For example, by precisely measuring variations within a field and adapting the strategy accordingly, farmers can greatly increase the effectiveness of pesticides and fertilisers and use them more judiciously.

- Fully autonomous robots like driverless tractors and weed-killing robots are taking over farms faster than anyone saw coming and becoming commercially available, which means machines will be able to spray, plant, plough and weed cropland. These machines are smaller and smarter than the gigantic machinery they aim to replace.

- The robots are precise: They distinguish the dull brown colour of diseased leaves from green vegetation and target chemicals directly at the weeds. In this way, a farmer can not only saves 80% of his chemical costs but saves the environment by using fewer chemicals.

- Advances in seed technology, fertilisers and other crop inputs led to high yields and over-supply. Farmers need to get to the next level of profitability and efficiency in farming. It is one of the main driving adoptions in agriculture, proving a better farming system and suggesting better ways to grow crops."

- Farmers can manage multiple tasks while being away from their farm; they can be on the phone and doing different things far away. There are some real opportunities there.

- Machinery that uses automation for tasks right now is more beneficial to farmers than autonomous equipment. Artificial intelligence, deep learning and
- advances in computer vision are going to transform agricultural machinery even further. Sensing and perception are one of the most challenging.
- A modern tractor does thousands of tasks, and to provide a fully autonomous solution, a deep understanding of each of those tasks is needed to automate them.

Role of SAAS-based cloud software in Smart Farming:

Cloud-based software is used for the management of financial and field activities of farms. Around the mid-2000s, satellite image use with Raven Receiver tools for field zone tracking became widely used. Farmers had to implement and coordinate with different tools to manage complete farm-operation. With constant improvements throughout the years, Agritech SaaS has become all in one tool to manage all these activities and more in one place through a single tool.

A good example is Cropin, working with the Government of Karnataka and leading multinational agro-corporations utilising data analytics and satellite imagery to collect, analyse data and manage all the activities from farm to fork. In March 2019 Cropin won the AI Innovation Challenge 2019, organised by the Government of Maharashtra and NITI Aayog, in association with NASSCOM.

Cropin is an intuitive, intelligent, self-evolving system that delivers future-ready farming solutions to the entire agricultural sector. It delivers decision-making tools that bring consistency, dependability and sustainability to agri-businesses. With live reporting capabilities, analysis, interpretation and insight that span across geographies, Cropin is digitising every farm, while data-managing the entire ecosystem. Smarter Agri-solutions powered in real-time; for farmers to archive patterns, predict trends, to make a blueprint for their business in the times to come.

"Making agriculture more predictable is the need of the hour, and only technological disruption can create impact at scale."

Krishna Kumar, CEO & Founder, Cropin.

Cropin's 'Smart Farm' technology platform has reached 5 million acres of farmland across 2 million farmers. At the back end, Cropin's data lake amplifies this ground-truth data with local weather information and high-resolution satellite imagery, which are the strong foundations of their AI-based solution platform called 'Smart Risk'.

By analysing and interpreting this data for the 265 crops with nearly 3,500 variants on its platform across billions of data points that grow every day, Cropin builds an agri-information highway that detects patterns and predicts the future of the crop highlighting the risk and opportunity for Agri stakeholders. Cropin provides near-real-time actionable insights to agriculture processors, distributors, inputs providers, lenders and insurers through its connector APIs. Additionally, Cropin's algorithms can establish every satellite image pixel's historic performance at the farm and regional level.

Cropin has also partnered with the Department of Agriculture (DOA), Government of Karnataka, to help farmers create more value for their crops. The project aims to assist 4.15 lakh farmers across 30 districts of Karnataka in digitising 3.4 lakh acres of farmlands.

Increase in efficiency:

Simplified data gathered through smartphone app records activities & indicators. It ensures efficient operations, lower costs and better visibility for field agents at all times

Scaling in productivity:

Real-time actionable insights enable farm management companies to take planned & responsive business decisions. The predictability of quantity & quality of yield combined with the reduced cost of input-operations results in higher productivity for the businesses

Strengthens Sustainability:

It meets today's agri-needs and strengthens resources for the future by creating a healthy environment, economic profitability and social & economic equity for all. It empowers the agri-businesses to benefit from actionable insights while empowering farmers through advisory & alerts.

How does it work?

Data Collection:

Cloud software stores tonnes of data relating to weather cycles, crop patterns, soil quality, harvesting and satellite imagery to provide insights with sharp accuracy and speed. So if in future, crops infected with the same symptoms as ten years ago, the data can be used to find the remedy used at that time.

Data Processing/Analysis:

Meteorological data, market data, farm data, GIS and water availability - all the data from past and present is analysed thoroughly before giving the optimum value of seeding, water and pesticide requirements for a farm. The systems also have an alert system whenever discrepancies in crop growth are detected. Hence these systems work efficiently in case of pest attack informing farmers with actionable data.

Data Storage and Dissemination:

Data storage is the backbone of predictive analysis. Earlier, the data storage was hardware-based. Nowadays, the Agri-tech systems are cloud-based, which means that one need not invest in the purchase and maintenance of hardware. All the data is available in clouds and can access through phone, PCs and tablets. Data storage is significant also inaccurate analysis. The more data is available relating to farms, the more accurate weather phenomena, pests, crop yield and profits will be.

Benefits of smart farming:

By making farming more connected and intelligent, precision agriculture helps reduce overall costs, improve the quality and quantity of products, and sustain agriculture. Increasing control overproduction leads to better cost-management and waste-reduction. The ability to trace anomalies in crop growth helps to eliminate the risk of losing yields. Additionally, automation boosts efficiency. With smart devices, multiple processes can activate at the same time, and automated services enhance product quality and volume by better controlling production processes.

The smart farming system helps manage the demand estimates and delivery of goods to market just in time to reduce waste.

Smart Farming- the future of agriculture:

Smart farming and IoT-driven agriculture are laying the groundwork for a "third green revolution," which refers to the combined application of information and communications technologies. It includes precision equipment, IoT sensors and actuators, geo-positioning systems, unmanned aerial vehicles (UAVs) and robots.

IoT technology helps better control agricultural processes to reduce production risks and enhance the ability to foresee production results, helping farmers better plan and distribute the product. Data about exact batches of crops and the number of crops to harvest can help farmers cut down on labour and waste.

Now the service providers and mobile operators are modernising their network infrastructure, bringing network resources to the edge. They integrate far distances through technologies such as small cells and massive MIMO to get ready for the 5G roll-out.

Overview

Smart Farming focuses on applying acquired data and combining it from various data sources to show the bigger picture to manage all the activities of the farm. Smart farming is a big leap from traditional farming as it brings certainty and predictability to the table. Robotics, automation and cloud software systems are tools for smart farming. Robotics, drones and sensor equipment placed throughout the farms can collect data, and this data is processed to produce farm insights. Cloud-based software can collect the data on farm and process the data relative to weather patterns, yields, irrigation and satellite imagery, and off-farm - such as markets and dealer availability to perform predictive analysis. Cloud-based software finds the applications for farmers, banks, food processing companies, insurance providers, seed production and government.

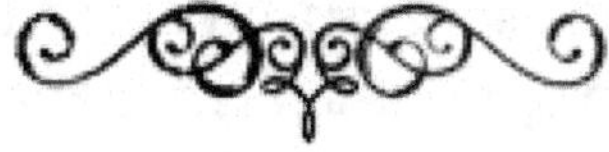

CHAPTER-8

FARM MANAGEMENT

Farm management means making and executing the decisions involved in organising and operating a farm for maximum production and profit. Farming has become a highly specialised activity. A farmer has to act like a good manager. As a farm manager, he has to plan, monitor and analyse all activities on-farm from Tillage, planting, crop protection, fertilisation, irrigation, harvesting to all other activities with minimum inputs, and cost-effectiveness. For this, he needs to track input usage quantities, costs and work hours for every activity.

In modern times, farmers are considering farming as a business rather than producing food for domestic consumption. Farm Management Software (FMS) helps

them optimise and provide more insight to manage complex agricultural operations. It is making them smarter from planning to harvest. This software is even customised to meet specific farm requirements as we know that each crop and each field has certain specific requirements. This software's beauty is to use with any mobile gadget, be it an android phone, tablets, i-pad, or windows.

Top Farm Management Software- Agrivi, Granular, Trimble, FarmERP, FarmLogs, Agword, Conservis are some of the top Farm Management Software (FMS).

Advantages of using Farm Management Software:

Farm Management Software connects a field to the office. It provides personalised guidance to farmers to put their plans into action. Farm managers can schedule and assign tasks to their workers. It saves time, reduces human error, and enables smart decisions that improve the bottom line. Farmers can see future prices benchmarked against daily price fluctuation. It leads to achieving objectives of profitable and sustainable agribusiness.

This software develops partners with farmers, crop advisors, agri-retailers, and food companies around the world. It enables growers, crop consultants, farm staff, precision specialists and operation managers to work as one.

The software helps any farmer to:

1. Develop a Crop Plan-

It provides a holistic view of the farm to plan farm activities efficiently. It gives an insight on when and how to conduct crop rotation, the most appropriate pest control method to use and the best fertiliser to apply.

2. Weather Monitoring & Pest Detection-

It helps in getting an instant overview of a 7-day weather forecast or 3-year history for every field. It alarms farmers if there is a risk of an insect pest or disease occurrence in their fields. With advanced insect pest and disease risk detection, farmers can apply on-time protection to crops.

3. Track and Measure field activities-

A big Farm has several employees that assist with the day to day operations of the business. These apps help them to send relevant information from the farm to the farm manager to oversee.

4. Resources & Real-time Inventory-

A Central record of employees, seasonal workers, machinery, and fields lets you keep control over your resources.

5. Farm Analytics & Reports-

It helps to identify why some crops grow better in some fields and determine the exact cost per unit for every variety per field. One can get all reports with a single click!

6. Manage Risk portfolios-

It helps to study the field performance in the past. A farmer can make informed decisions on which crop to invest in and which one to avoid. It also helps to understand input cost, project yields, sale-prices, external risks such as erratic weather conditions, disease, pests, and unpredictable market demands beyond farmers' control are part of the challenges modern farmers have to deal with.

7. Farm Economics-

The software helps farmers keep farm financial records and documents in one place, track sales, expenses, and capital investments and allocate them to each crop production. Farmers do not miss their payments with due date alarms!

8. Forecast and measure profits-

Like any other business, farmers should keep track of all the expenses and any activity carried out on the farm. FMS helps to keep track of all financial activities to improve efficiency and boost productivity.

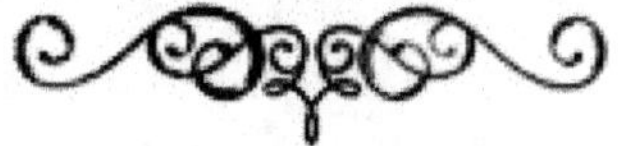

CHAPTER-9

STORAGE

India ranks 94 out of 107 countries in Global Hunger Index (GHI) in 2020 and more importantly, ranks 72 out of 113 in countries in the Global Food Security Index (GFSI) because of poor post-harvest management of food which leads to loss of availability of food (worth 92651 crores) before it reaches the end customer. It is approximately 40% of India's total production, making India one of the few countries to have higher post-harvest losses. According to the UN's FAO report, globally, around 1.3 billion metric tons of food, 33% of the total produce is lost in the post-harvest stage.

Post-harvest loss (PHL) is a critical issue- Food is available for human consumption from harvesting to consumption but goes unconsumed termed as "Food loss".

It is mainly due to a lack of knowledge, inadequate technology and/or poor storage infrastructure. Food loss in the supply chain reduced using advanced technologies and efficient crop handling and storage systems.

Need for Scientific methods for Storage:

Produce Storage is of all-time concern for man to reserve food supply to mitigate hunger at a future date. It is an important marketing function involving holding and preserving foods from the time they produced until they needed it. It ensures a continuous flow of foods in the market.

Storage protects the quality of perishable and semi-perishable products from deterioration.

Some of the farm products have seasonal demand. To cope with this demand, production continuously and storage becomes necessary. It helps in the stabilization of prices by adjusting demand and supply.

Storage is necessary for some period for the performance of other marketing functions. Storage provides employment and income through price advantages.

Indian Warehousing Market:

Major players operating in the warehousing market include Container Corporation of India Ltd., Gati Ltd., Mahindra Logistics Ltd., Transport Corporation of India Ltd., Central Warehousing Corporation, DHL Express (India) Pvt. Ltd., Jayem Warehousing Pvt. Ltd., JICS Logistics Ltd., Shalimar Warehousing Corporation, Spear Logistics Pvt. Ltd., among others. Three public sector agencies involved in building large-scale storage and warehousing capacities in the country are-

Food Corporation of India (FCI) has the largest agricultural warehousing systems with over 758.46 million tonnes of storage capacity in over 1820 godowns located all over India.

Central Warehousing Corporation (CWC) was founded in 1957 to provide logistics support to the agricultural sector. As a premier Warehousing Agency, CWC operates

421 warehouses as of 01.10.2020 with a total operational storage capacity of100.26 LMT. It aims to provide reliable, cost-effective, value-added, integrated warehousing and logistics solution in a socially responsible and environmentally friendly manner. It offers services such as disinfestations, pest-control, fumigation, handling and transportation, procurement and distribution.

State Warehousing Corporations (SWCs) exist in 17 States to provide storage facilities and pest control services for various agricultural commodities belonging to that state's farmers. These warehouses work under different Warehousing Acts enacted by the respective State Governments.

While the FCI uses its warehouses mainly for storing food grains, the storage capacities with CWC and SWCs used to store food grains and other items.

Uses of Warehouses-

- It helps in scientific storage of produce from the vagaries of weather, rodents, insects and pests. They prevent quality and quantity losses.
- It meets the financial needs of people who store the produce by providing value for the goods stored.
- It helps in regulating price levels. More goods from the buffer are released when supplies are less and less is released when supplies are more in the markets.
- Offers market intelligence in the form of price, supply and demand information so that market users may develop selling and buying strategies.

Growth in the warehousing sector

According to a study, the Indian Warehousing Market expected to be an estimated $12.2 billion in 2020, growing to $19.5 billion by 2025. The warehousing market is driven by the country's manufacturing, retail, FMCG and logistics sectors. Furthermore, supportive government policies such as establishing logistic parks and free trade warehouse zones may spur market growth through 2025. GST has led to a reduction in inventory and turnaround time, which has led to the removal of checkpoints, thereby diminishing state boundaries.

Besides, technological advancements such as the advent of AI, IoT, 3D-Printing, among others, in the warehousing industry need to create lucrative opportunities over the next few years. Moreover, the emergence of third-party logistics and super grid logistics may fuel the market growth during the forecast period.

Further, the sudden outbreak and spread of COVID-19 have a short-term impact on warehousing demand due to lockdown and reduced manufacturing activities. Further, it will help strengthen the warehousing industry in India on account of the shifting consumer preference from an offline mode of shopping to online to adhere to the social distancing norms.

Segmentation of warehouses

The Indian Warehousing Market is segmented based on type, ownership, sector, usage pattern, infrastructure, end-user industry, company and region.

Based on type, the market can be segmented into general, speciality and refrigerated. The refrigerated segment can witness significant growth due to the rising demand for such warehouses to store perishable food items and ensure food security & safety.

Based on ownership, the market categorized into public, private and bonded. The government and semi-government agencies own the public ownership segment. Such warehouses aid (rent) the small traders who do not have their warehouses.

Based on the usage pattern, the market split into single and co-warehousing segments. There is a preference increasing for co-warehousing among manufacturers,

suppliers, logistic companies as well as startups. Co-warehousing provides flexible storage that can help businesses meet their needs and give them better control over their budgets. Co-warehousing provides scalability and helps in reducing overall operational costs.

Communal Ware House:

Where farmers come together in groups, they often consider establishing communal stores that a trained store manager manages. The individual farmers can consolidate their stocks ready for the market by delivering to the communal store. This arrangement may be the better option for smallholder farmers who do not have the capital to put up own stores, have limitations of land available for the store or do not know how to store commodity well for extended periods.

These stores work extremely well as bulking centres where large traders come and pickup truck loads of commodity (preferably of the same quality) at one time. The advantage to the big buyer is the reduction in buying through multiple aggregate traders with their multiplied handling costs.

Modern storage structures:

Silos are used in agriculture for bulk storage of grain. Three types of silos are in widespread use today: tower silos, bunker silos, and bag silos. Silos are made from steel or concrete. Metal ones are costlier but are easier to erect. Both are sturdy and keep the food grain safe for a long time.

Transportation naturally plays a major role in influencing the design of a silo. One can have silos with rail connectivity (cost around Rs 50-60 crores for 50,000-tonne capacity) that makes the task of transportation very efficient or standalone silos without rail connectivity. The grain transported using trucks of various sizes and capacity. These cost around Rs 30 crores for 50,000-tonne capacity.

A silo is an ideal storage mode for a country like India, which depends heavily on buffer stock for food capacity. It has proven to be beneficial for all stakeholders: farmers, government, procurement agencies, etc.

India first started using modern silos in the 1990s, but its real value realized only now, and large capacity silos built by the government and private companies. Metal silos regarded as too costly for small scale storage. Nevertheless, certain projects have been successful in introducing small metal silos, of 0.4 to 10-tonne capacity, at farm/village level in developing countries

Silos vs warehouses:

- Very large storage capacity; 25,000 to 50,000 tonnes and beyond

- Low running costs due to larger quantities
- Low labour requirements due to high level of mechanization
- Rapid handling, saving time
- Low wastage through spillage and rodents
- Effective and efficient fumigation operation
- Less land area requirement covers one-third space horizontally of warehouses
- Complete control of aeration
- Possible to store the grain for very long periods
- Possible to mechanize all operations
- Possible to store moist grain for short periods
- Complete protection against natural elements

According to the high-level Dalwai committee report, the financial investment is required to improve storage and transportation facilities for food crops. Except for cold storage, the country is lagging in all other agri-logistics required to bring the produce from farm to markets. If plugged, the sector can create over 3 million jobs, a majority of which will be at the village level

There is a need for more widespread education to farmers on the causes of post-harvest losses and the costs and benefits of the grain storage structures; they are currently using. Farmers need to be provided with information on how much they lose during storage to make more informed decisions when investing in grain storage structures.

The use of the metal silo, which is more feasible for grain storage, should be promoted. However, the cost of the metal silo is prohibitive for most small scale farmers, which may slow down its adoption. Without credit provision to these farmers, farmers may take longer to shift from the traditional storage structures to new technologies like the metal silo.

Financial support is therefore needed to enable farmers to acquire the metal silos. Moreover, technical training must be accompanied by the development of business management and entrepreneurship skills.

Cold chains and Refrigeration:

Refrigeration can substantially reduce the rate at which food will deteriorate. Low temperatures slow down the growth of microorganisms and the rate of chemical (including enzymatic) changes in food.

Availability of proper cold storages is important for preserving perishable commodities like milk, meat, eggs, vegetables, fruits, ornamental flowers and other floricultural goods. These cold storages give perishable food items a longer shelf life by preventing them from rotting due to humidity, high temperature and micro-organisms. Small thermochromic data loggers can be put into strategically chosen boxes (cartons) clearly marked with Alert Tape when sending perishable goods.

What Are Perishable Foods?

Perishable foods consist of fresh vegetables, and fruits are stored in cold storage or refrigerator to increase their lives. Perishable food products, even when they are optimally processed and packaged, have a limited shelf life. A cost-efficient way to monitor the temperature conditions of food products individually throughout distribution is required to indicate their real quality state indirectly.

India is the second-largest producer of fruits and

vegetables in the world with a combined production of about 210 million metric tons per year. A study by the Central Institute of Post-Harvest Engineering and Technology (CIPHET), Ludhiana, reports that about 18% of fruits and vegetables are lost in the post-harvest.

Existing Problems in Cold Chain:

Cold storage infrastructure is one of the most important factors in the post-harvest process. There are about 7600 cold storages in India that account for 34.9 million metric tons of storage capacity, but their distribution is not equally spread among the states. Around 59% of the storage capacity is present only in Punjab, Uttar Pradesh, Madhya Pradesh and Gujarat. Of the cold storages, 96% are privately run, and government bodies, institution and co-operatives run the rest. About 75% of the cold stores are dedicated only to potatoes which signify the dearth of availability to other products. About 5000 cold stores were built much before having no integrated pack houses or ancillary units to assist food storage.

Most of these cold stores are located near the production centres and thus depend heavily on transportation to reach the consumers. According to estimates, India transports around 104 million metric tons of fruits and vegetables every year. However, only 4 million metric tons are transported through refrigerated vans (reefers); the rest are transported through non-refrigerated trucks and vans.

What are the benefits of Cold Storage for storing Perishables?

There are many advantages of cold storage when used for

storing perishable foods. Some of them are discussed further:

- Lowers Deterioration Rate of Perishable Foods
- Temperature Controls
- Lowers the Risk of Food Poisoning
- Minimizes the Hassle of Cooking on Regular Intervals
- Enables to Store Foods for a Longer period

The vegetables and fruits are categorized as fresh perishable produce that needs the fastest transport with storage at receiving front-end.

It should also be noted that the fresh perishables must not be stored at production centres but moved to demand-side while still young and firm to withstand rigours of transport. It is here that the Indian Railways with its pan-India network is the optimal and preferred choice for movement of horticultural produce. This burgeoning demand is not fully tapped or planned for in full pointed out the Dalwai committee report on post-production agri-logistics.

The Future of Transport Refrigeration and Climate-Control Technology:

The perishable food transport industry has reached a point where the next advances will involve sanitary transportation, telematics, and computerized refrigeration systems. Advances will concentrate on how perishable food products can be safely and economically transported to markets with the best possible retention of wholesomeness, eating quality, and nutritional quality for consumers, no matter where they reside.

Future refrigerated equipment will most likely be complete climate control systems equipped with telematics, expert systems, feedback systems, and traceability.

The refrigerated equipment will in all probability allow for remote management, control, and recording of multiple microenvironments such as temperature; humidity; O_2; CO_2; N_2; and volatile organic compounds, including ethylene; as well as mould spores and pathogenic bacteria.

It understands that an end goal of transport systems is to maintain the initial condition and extend the shelf life of wholesome perishable foods.

There are significant opportunities for future developments in climate control management to establish prediction models for managing the shelf life of produce and other perishable items. Sensor control data to commodity physiology will allow for the early detection of physiological or pathological disorders, as well as residual shelf-life prediction modelling with models that are unique to each product.

Soon, transport refrigeration and atmosphere control systems will minimize microbiological food safety risks by utilizing technologies for sanitizing the container and cargo based on the recorded microbial load.

To illustrate, sanitizing the air circulating within the components and conditioned space of reefer equipment could reduce the presence of food spoilage and food poisoning organisms from the air and the surface of the refrigerated equipment components as the cargo. It will leave no negative effect on the commodity or humans as long as the process is validated, monitored, and controlled.

In the future, information about the condition of the products being transported will be continuously available to stakeholders in real-time with remote temperature management systems and satellite communication. The technology is available now to accomplish this.

Future use of distributed sensor arrangements combined with real-time remote monitoring and control systems will provide holistic and robust tools for the effective management of refrigerated transport.

Programs that allow for predicting the remaining shelf life of a product will allow receivers to make accept/reject decisions in real-time without delayed download, as with traditional temperature data loggers.

Cold chains situation in India:

Farmers often have excess fruits and vegetables that

cannot be consumed immediately but would store well. Stored fruits and vegetables harvested at peak maturity from the farm usually have better flavour and a higher nutritional value. It is important to remember that crops held in storage are still living plants, capable of respiration and affected by their environment. The goal of storage is to keep them in a dormant state.

The state of cold storage in the country is better than other storage methods. However, it should be underlined that the existing cold storage capacity is confined mostly to certain crop types and not integrated with other requirements.

Close to only 16 per cent of the target set for creating integrated pack-houses, reefer trucks, and cold storage and ripening units have been met. There is a gap of 84-99 per cent in achieving the target of improving the state of storage and transportation of the farm produce.

Out of these, the country is far-far behind in meeting the requirement of integrated pack-houses, reefer trucks and ripening units. Use late-maturing varieties better suited to storage.

Opportunities and Way Forward:

The supply chain management and the cold storage is highly organised for milk which has resulted in very fewer losses. Much of this success is due to the success of Amul Co-operative in Gujarat. Amul collects milk from farmers at advanced collection centres after testing it for milk-fat

content. The milk is then transferred to chilling centres where it is cooled at four °C and then transported to processing plants and distribution centres in insulated tankers. It is imperative to have such technologically advanced and organised process for fruits and vegetables to reduce the losses.

India would need another 30 million metric tons of storage that is distributed evenly throughout different states of the country. The ripening units for processing fruits and vegetables currently stand at 812 units while the country requires 9000 units to be at par with what is consumed today.

Advanced control and monitoring technology for fruits in storage will help extend their shelf life and decrease the wastage while also promoting multi-commodity cold storages that can help in easier and distributed storage to a wide range of commodity the urban centres.

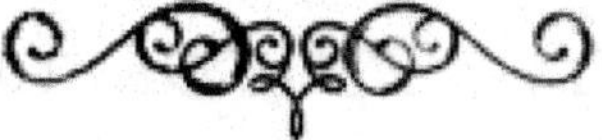

CHAPTER-10

PROFITABLE UTILIZATION OF AGRICULTURAL WASTES

Agricultural development is usually accompanied by wastes from the irrational application of intensive farming methods and the abuse of chemicals used in cultivation. These wastes are non-product outputs of production and processing of agri-products that may contain material that can benefit man but whose economic values are less than the cost of collection, transportation, and processing for beneficial use.

What is Agricultural waste?

Agricultural wastes are the residues from the growing and processing of raw agricultural products such as fruits, vegetables and crops. Agricultural waste or agro-waste is

comprised of animal waste (manure, animal carcasses), food processing waste, crop waste (stalks, sugarcane bagasse, drops and culls from fruits and vegetables, pruning) and hazardous and toxic agricultural waste (pesticides, insecticides and herbicides, etc.).

Expanding agricultural production has naturally resulted in increased quantities of agricultural crop residues and agro-industrial by-products.

There is likely to be a significant increase in agricultural wastes globally if developing countries continue to intensify farming systems. It is estimated that about 998 million tonnes of agricultural waste are produced yearly. Organic wastes can amount up to 80 per cent of the total solid wastes generated in any farm of which manure production can amount up to 5.27 kg/day/1000 kg live weight, on a wet weight basis.

Agricultural waste management system (AWMS):

An Agricultural Waste Management System (AWMS) is a "planned system in which all necessary components are installed and managed to control and use byproducts of agricultural production in a manner that sustains or enhances the quality of air, water, soil, plant, and animal resources". Such a system is developed using a total systems approach, i.e. it is designed to cater to all the waste associated with agricultural production to utilization throughout the year-round.

Why is Agricultural Waste Management important?

"For a healthy life, one needs quality food, water and air. Quality food means nutritive food free from pollutants. It comes from healthy soil. Quality air and water means ones free from any contamination/pollutants." If not managed properly, agricultural waste from farm operations can pollute the environment. It impacts water quality and general aesthetics. This degradation reduces the ability of adjacent waterways and groundwater resources to support aquatic life. The water becomes unfit for human and animal consumption. Nitrates, from fertilizers and agricultural waste runoff, can seep into groundwater. This water contaminated with nitrates is hazardous to humans as it results in oxygen depletion in the blood. Thus, proper waste management can reduce operating costs associated with fertilizer application.

Agricultural waste management makes good sense both environmentally and economically. It intends to make use of nutrients available in wastes for maximizing crop production and minimizing environmental pollution.

Advantages of Waste Management:

Like most other aspects of agricultural production, there are requirements for applying and managing agricultural waste on farms. It is a plan developed for a farm to benefit crop production and minimize environmental impact. Site-specific waste management strategies can maximize cost-efficiency.

Usually, agricultural waste is discharged into the environment with or without treatment. There is a need to consider waste as potential resources rather than undesirable and unwanted, avoid contamination of air, water, and land resources, and avoid transmission of hazardous materials. It will require better use of technology and incentives, a change in philosophy and attitudes, and better agricultural waste management approaches.

Agricultural waste utilization technology must either use the residues rapidly or store the residues under conditions that do not cause spoilage or render the residues unsuitable for processing to the desired end.

1. Manure:

Adding manure to soil increases its fertility because it increases the nutrient retention capacity, improves the physical condition, the water- holding capacity and the soil structure stability. Farm-Yard Manure is decomposed mixture of dung, urine. Compost from Farm is made from refuse like weeds, crop stubble, straw, cotton stalks, groundnut husks, leaves, sugarcane trash, hedge clippings, litter, etc. Phospho-compost materials from organic/vegetable waste/straw, cow-dung (dry weight), and phosphate rock are used. Vermicompost involves earthworms, which eat biomass and release it as excreta. Vermicompost is considered superior due to having more bacteria and plant growth-promoting substances. Therefore, the earthworm is considered as "pulse of the soil" and "healthier the pulse, healthier the soil". It ensures the availability of all essential nutrients in a larger amount. Crop residues/weed mulch, wood ashes, and supplying nutrients to the current crop leave a substantial residual effect on succeeding crops. Non-edible oil-cakes are not fed to cattle and therefore, can be used as manure, especially for horticultural crops.

2. Electricity Generation:

Make Electricity from organic waste substances like waste wood, straw, husk, polythene, plastic, rubber, leather, waste clothes, waste paper, etc.

3. Produce second-generation biofuels:

Biofuel like ethanol and gas can be extracted from straw, oil industries waste liquids, plastics and bagasse. The biogas made in biogas plants is mostly used in cooking. The methane gas generated by biogas plants can also be used for heating, lighting and motive powers. Biogas slurry has comparatively more nutrients than FYM.

4. Anaerobic Digestion:

Methane gas can be produced from agricultural wastes, particularly manures. The gas is best suited for heating purposes as broiler operation, water heating, grain drying, etc. It stabilizes the waste, and the digestion sludge is relatively odour-free and yet retains the original waste's fertiliser value.

5. Adsorbents in the Elimination of Heavy Metals:

Due to industrialization and urbanization, heavy metals are released into the environment and causing a great problem worldwide. Unlike organic pollutants, most of which are susceptible to biological degradation, heavy metal ions such as copper, cadmium, mercury, zinc, chromium and lead ions do not degrade into harmless end products.

The presence of heavy metal ions is a major concern. The toxicity to many life forms. The low-cost agricultural waste includes sugarcane bagasse, rice husk, sawdust, coconut husk, oil palm shell, neem bark, etc., for eliminating heavy metals from wastewater have been investigated by various researchers.

6. Pyrolysis:

In pyrolysis systems, agricultural waste heated up to 400-600°C in the absence of oxygen to vaporize a portion of the material, leaving a char behind. It is considered to be a higher technology procedure for the utilization of agricultural wastes. Others are hydro-gasification and hydrolysis. They are used for the preparation of chemicals from agricultural waste as well as for energy recovery. Of particular interest to agriculture are the preparation of alcohols for fuel, ammonia for fertilizers, glucose for food and feed. Pyrolysis of agricultural waste yields oil, char and low heating value gas.

7. Animal feed:

In most developing countries, the problem with animal feed is limited availability of protein sources, although great efforts are being made to find alternative supplements. Crop residues have high fibre content and are low in protein, starch and fat. It can be circumvented by utilizing residues to feed domesticated animals.

Agricultural Waste Management System (AWMS) consist of production, collection, storage, treatment, transfer, and utilization:

- Production is a function of the amount and nature of agricultural waste generated. The waste requires management if quantities produced is sufficient enough to become a resource concern

- Collection refers to the initial capture and gathering of the generated waste from the point of origin. Storage has to do with the temporary containment or holding of the waste. The storage facility of a waste management system provides control over the scheduling and timing of treatment and application or waste disposal.

- Treatment is any function designed to reduce the waste's pollution or toxic potential, including physical, biological, and chemical treatment and increases its potential beneficial use.

- The transfer is the movement and transportation of the waste from the collection to the utilization stage either as a solid, liquid, or slurry, depending on the total solids concentration.

- Utilization is the application of the waste for beneficial use, and it includes recycling reusable waste products and reintroducing non-reusable waste products into the environment.

The '3R' Approach to Agricultural waste management system (AWM)

Waste minimization efficiency is stated to be better achieved by applying 3Rs in a hierarchical order- Reduce Reuse and Recycle.

- The concept of minimizing waste reduces the quantity and ill-effects of waste generation by reducing the number of wastes, reusing the waste products with simple treatments and recycling the wastes by using it as resources to produce same or modified products. This is usually referred to as '3R'.
- Some waste products can be consumed as resources for producing different goods or the same product, meaning recycling the same resource.
- When wastes are reused time and again, it offsets harvesting of new similar or same products. It saves fresh resources exploitation and reduces waste generation.

All in all, the 3Rs individually or collectively saves fresh resources exploitation, add value to the already exploited resources and very importantly minimizes the waste quantity and its ill effects. The principle of reducing waste, reusing and recycling resources and products (3Rs) aims at achieving efficient minimization of waste generation.

Overview

Agricultural wastes, when managed properly through the application of the knowledge of agricultural waste management systems such as the "3Rs" can be transformed into beneficial materials for human and agricultural usage. It is important to note from the findings that proper waste collections, storage, treatment, transfer, and utilization are a panacea to a healthy environment.

CHAPTER-11

AGRICULTURAL CO-OPERATIVES DEVELOPMENT

A co-operative, being an association of many small farmers, acts as a large business entity in the market. The Indian cooperative movement was formally launched in India in 1904. Hence, the co-operative organisations have proved instrumental in the development of the agricultural and rural sectors in particular by combining the merits of both the public and the private players. Three typical examples are a machinery pool, a marketing co-operative, and a credit union.

In agricultural co-operative small and marginal farmers pool their resources to protect their ways of life and secure their livelihoods. Co-operatives are essentially voluntary associations of people with common economic, social and cultural needs, and aspirations. These are largely autonomous and are jointly owned and democratically

controlled by its members. In co-operatives, the profits are consolidated, kept with and shared between all the members themselves. Co-operative organisations help make loans at reasonable interest rates, procure and provide manure, seeds, pesticides, and other agricultural implements to the farmers.

It is seen that co-operative organisations have immense potential in delivering goods and services where both government and private players were unable to do so. Moreover, many such organisations form self-help groups and contribute to rural and agricultural development in the social, communal and economic sectors.

Various co-operatives had even taken initiatives for promoting and practising Agro-Forestry by combining the plantations of medicinal plants, fruit and forest trees to contribute towards improving the ecology and overall climate of the wastelands.

India is a witness to the commendable success of co-operatives includes the Indian Farmers Fertiliser Cooperative Ltd. (IFFCO), the Krishak Bharti Fertiliser Cooperative Ltd. (KRIBHCO), National Co-operative Development Corporation (NCDC), National Agricultural Co-operative Marketing Federation of India (NAFED), Indian Farmers Fertilisers Co-operative Limited (IFFCO), Co-operative Rural Development Trust (CORDET), and National Bank for Agriculture and Rural Development INAHARD).

Types of Agricultural Cooperatives:

There are two primary types of agricultural service cooperatives, supply cooperative and marketing cooperative.

Supply cooperatives supply their members with inputs for agricultural production, including seeds, fertilizers, fuel, and machinery services.

Farmers establish marketing cooperatives to undertake transformation, packaging, distribution, and marketing of farm products (both crop and livestock).

Farmers also widely rely on credit cooperatives as a source of financing for both working capital and investments.

Why farmers prefer to form co-operatives?

A practical motivation for the creation of agricultural co-operatives is *"overcoming the curse of smallness"*. A family farm may be too small to justify the purchase of a tractor or another piece of farm machinery for its use; a machinery pool co-operative purchases the necessary equipment for the joint use of all its members as needed.

A small farm does not always have the means of transportation necessary for delivering its products to the market. Furthermore, the small volume of its production may put it in an unfavourable negotiating position to intermediaries and wholesalers; a cooperative will act as an integrator, collecting its small members' output and delivering it in large aggregated quantities downstream through the marketing channels.

A small farmer may be charged relatively high-interest rates by commercial banks, mindful of high transaction costs on small loans. These banks may refuse credit to small farmers due to lack of collateral. At the same time, A farmers' credit union will be able to raise loan at lower rates from commercial banks because of the large size of the cooperative. Then distribute loans to its members on the strength of mutual or peer-pressure guarantees for repayment.

The agriculture credit societies:

The organization of these societies dates back to 1904 when the first Co-operative Societies Act was passed. These societies were started with the object of providing cheap credit to the agriculturists to free them from the clutches of the greedy money-lenders. The agricultural primary credit society is the foundation-stone on which the whole co-operative network relies. The first Agricultural Credit Society in the Firozpur District was registered on 4 October 1911, at the Village of Khalchi Kadim in the Firozpur Tehsil.

At the State level, the Punjab State co-operative Supply and Marketing Federation (MARKFED) is playing an important role in building up an integrated structure for remunerative marketing and storing agricultural produce. It has played an important role in accelerating the Green Revolution in the State by arranging ready supplies of essential farm inputs needed by the cultivators.

Working of Co-operative farming societies:

The Royal Commission on Agriculture in 1928 observed that if co-operation failed, it would fail the hope of the Indian agriculturist. Co-operative farming is a compromise between collective farming and the peasant proprietorship and gives all merits of large-scale farming without abolishing private property. It implies an organization of the farmers based on common efforts for common interests. Under this system, all landowners in a village form a co-operative society for tilling the land. The land is pooled, but each farmer retains the right of property. Each distributes the produce. They are allowed to withdraw from the co-operative farm whenever they desire. In India, the exceedingly small size of holdings is perhaps the most serious defect in our agriculture. If agriculture has to be improved, the size of the holdings must be enlarged.

The Indian Co-operative Movement has earned the distinction of being the largest in the world. There are about 5.5 lakhs of cooperative Societies with a membership of more than 22 crores. It covers a wide range of commercial activities, and nearly 50% of them are engaged in agriculture and agriculture-related matters. Nearly 70% of the Indian population is dependent on agriculture, is thus, connected with agricultural Co-operatives.

Co-operatives have covered 100% of villages and 67% of rural households. The co-operative sector contributes 50% of total agricultural credit and distributes 35% of total fertilizer consumption. They are procuring 60% of total sugar-cane. They are also playing a crucial role in the agro-processing sector, i.e. processing sugar-cane, milk, cotton and oilseeds etc.

Challenges before co-operatives:

Today, the Co-operatives are at the crossroad of their existence. Fast-emerging economic liberalization and globalization is a challenge for their existence. Despite being largest movement in the world and strongest link, it faces many challenges like lack of internal resources and poor mobilization of external resources, inadequate infrastructure, competitive tier structure, the apathy of members towards management, lack of accountability, increasing sickness, dormancy, low-level professionalism, excessive government control, political interference, the dominance of vested interest over the management, lack of human resources development, education and training and so on.

Despite all challenges, Co-operatives have to be sustainable over a time for which professionalism is essential. Co-operatives have been looking for Governmental help.

Nevertheless, they have been paying it off like official domination and interference in their day-to-day working etc.

Dr Kuriyan, an eminent co-operator in the country said

"The Co-operatives have undergone a crisis of identity is neither the government nor private. Co-operatives need to be more efficient and competitive, but at the same time, they cannot sacrifice the basic tenets of co-operation. Inefficient Co-operatives will have to either pull up their socks or down their shutters."

Co-operatives have many advantages in tackling problem of poverty alleviation, employment generation and food security. They also can deliver goods and services in areas where both the State and Private sectors have failed.

Despite all these, no doubt, the Co-operatives have contributed a lot to the country's agriculture development. We cannot afford to see that these institutions wither away.

Reforms:

- It needs reforms like timely conduct of elections, audit, general body meetings, and the right of a member for access to information and the management's accountability.
- Co-operatives need to be member-driven; stakeholders should have a command over its affairs and activities. There is a need for more transparency, more interaction and confidence-building measures. An aggressive marketing strategy should be adopted for sensitizing members about the service and quality rendered by the Co-operatives.

- Commitment to best service and pursuit for excellence should be the hallmark of Co-operative. Every society should adapt their customers' or members' charter and should meticulously adhere

to this charter.

- Co-operative should compete with other players in prevailing market forces. Strengthening information and database of Co-operatives should be of utmost importance. MIS need to be adopted by computerization and interconnectivity to provide best services to members and customers.
- Professionalization of management is one of the basic prerequisites of Co-operatives. Both the personnel and directors of a committee of management should be exposed to regular training, interaction and orientation.
- Adopting scientific planning for deployment of human resources on the principle of 'right man for the right post at the right time' would help Co-operatives accelerate the pace of reforms.
- Human resources need to be proactive. Motivation, recognition for good work and leadership should be inculcated for augmenting productivity.
- Basic tenets of corporate governance are adopted like fair play, transparency and accountability.

Cooperative Credit in Agriculture Development:

Nowadays, credit serves as an elevator. It has been recognized as the lifeblood of all economic activities. Like all other producers, agriculturists also need credit. According to an old proverb, "credit supports the farmers as the hangman's rope supports the hanged." This Statement is fully true in the context of Indian farmers. Thus, for stimulating the tempo of agricultural production, an adequate and timely credit is essential.

The Co-operative Societies Act, 1904 gave concretized shape for establishing primary co-operative societies. It will help to meet both the short and medium-term loan needs of farmers. The provision of these loans did not improve and did not impact the farmer's socioeconomic status, and consequently, they were head and ears in debt. To solve this problem and make the farmers free from the cruel clutches of money lenders, the idea of co-operative long-term credit institutions called Co-operative Agricultural, and Rural Development Banks/Co-operative Gram Vikas Banks (earlier called Cooperative Land Development/Mortgage Banks) was mooted.

Agricultural Cooperative in China:

China passed its first comprehensive Agricultural Cooperative Law in 2006, which became effective in July 2007. Since then, the incorporation of agricultural cooperatives in China has grown rapidly, emanating primarily from two sources: grassroots initiatives and government promotion. By August of 2013, there were 885,700 agricultural cooperatives in China. On average, over 10,000 agricultural cooperatives are incorporated each month under this new law. This organizational form grew to 1.52% of the entire number of business firms in China by August 2013.

Agricultural Cooperative in Israel:

Israel's agriculture is highly organized into farm societies. One society, the Farmer's Federation, has a membership of 7,000 citrus growers. There are plantation development companies and associations of wine, fruit, milk, and cotton producers. A unique feature of the management of agriculture in Israel is its two types of cooperative settlements.

Moshav:

A moshav is a village containing up to 150 farm family units and supported by a strong multipurpose cooperative organization. Each family is an economic and social unit, living in its own house and managing and working its fields.

Although each farm family is independent, its social and economic security is ensured by the village's cooperative structure, whose organization markets the produce, purchases the farm and household equipment, and provides the farmer with credit and other services.

Kibbutz:

A kibbutz, numbering from 60 to 2,000 members, is a true collective based on common ownership of resources and on pooling of labour and income; it functions as a single democratic unit. Under the supervision of a manager, each member performs an assigned task but receives no salary or wages, because the kibbutz provides all the members' needs.

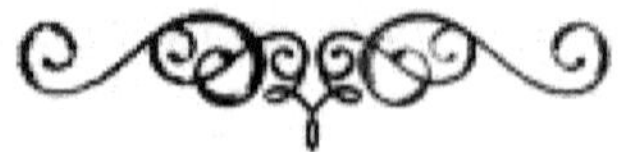

CHAPTER-12

FARMER PRODUCER COMPANIES

Farmer Producer Organisations are typically defined as "membership-based organisations or federations of organisations with elected leaders accountable to their constituents". These organisations have an objective to develop and deploy the aggregation mechanism of farmers, wherein farmers/producers with common interest agree to pool their resources to form a group. They jointly deal with various farming issues; be it credit, input sourcing, deployment of farm technology and good agricultural practices, post-harvest handling or onward sale of agricultural produce".

A Farmer Producer Company is a hybrid between co-operative societies and private limited companies. A Producer Company is a corporate body registered as a private limited company under Part IX-A of Companies Act 1956, now 2013 (as amended in 2002). An amendment in Companies Act 2002 was done based on the recommendation of Y. K. Alagh Committee (1998) to add corporate muscle to cooperatives to bring effective management and good governance. The same provisions have been retained for FPCs after revisiting the Companies Act in 2013.

The main objective of the formation of FPC is to help in doubling farmers' income and establish basic business principles within farming communities, bring industry and agriculture closer, and boost rural development by collectivisation of farmers, especially small and marginal farmers. India's first Farmer Producer Company was the Vanilla India Producer Co. in Kerala (est. 2004).

Objective:

- The primary objective of mobilising farmers into member-owned producer organisations, or FPOs, is to enhance farmers' production, productivity, and profitability, especially small and marginal farmers.
- They are owned and governed by shareholder farmers (or artisans) and administered by professional managers.
- They adopt all the good principles of co-operatives and the efficient business practices of companies and seek to address the cooperative structure's
inadequacies.
- They are related to all or any of the following matters: Production, Harvesting, Procurement, Grading, Pooling, Handling, Marketing, Selling and Import/Export of primary produce.

On 31.10.2019, against a target of 8.85 lakh farmers to be mobilised, 8.28 lakh small and marginal farmers have been identified and aggregated into 822 FPOs. They have been registered while 80 are under the process of registration. More recently, in the Union budget of 2019-20, the Government of India has announced its intention to promote

10,000 FPOs in the next five years to ensure economies of scale for farmers in the country.

Accordingly, the Small Farmers Agribusiness Consortium (SFAC) has prepared a strategy to scale up the number of FPOs virtually catalysing an FPO movement in the country. Over some time, every small and marginal farmer will eventually be a part of this movement.
A Producer Company must be formed by:

- Ten or more individuals each of them being Producers; or by
- Two or more Producer institutions; or by
- A combination of 10 or more individuals and Producer institutions

Advantages of FPOs: Numerous reports and studies have captured and established the positive role of FPOs. Some of the important benefits ascribed to FPOs are as under:

- Cost of production or cultivation may be reduced by procuring all necessary inputs in Bulk at wholesale rates and the use of custom hiring services of farm equipment.
- Therefore, aggregation of produce and bulk transport reduces marketing cost, enhancing the producer's net value accruals.
- Building scale through the aggregation of commodities lends economies of scale and attracts traders, processors, and retailers to the farm gate.
- Access to modern technology, extension services and joint training on Good Agricultural Practices (GAP) and ensuring agriculture traceability produce. Post-harvest losses can be minimised through joint storage and value add-

ition facilities.

- Adverse price fluctuations and distress sale can be managed or avoided; if good practices are imbibed. These include contract farming agreements, stocking in own common facilities or leased storage facilities with credit support, etc.
- Ease in communication to disseminate information about prices and volumes in different locations and other farming-related advisories, thereby reducing information asymmetries.
- Access to institutional credit against a stock, without collateral by joint liability implicit in the FPO framework.
- Movement up the value chain and graduation into primary and secondary processing will be possible as minimum scale economies are reaped.
- Greater bargaining power to farmers and greater quality orientation in production and processing activities.
- The Farmer Producer companies have democratic governance, each producer or member has equal voting rights irrespective of the number of shares held.
- There is a limitation on the amount that can be distributed as a dividend. Profit is largely distributed based on "patronage", which acts as a reward for members contributing to the business.
- There can be 5-15 directors, and expert directors can be co-opted for professional guidance.

As a result of the above initiatives, farmer members of the

FPOs are saving in production and commission cost, and there is reduced wastage of produce and value addition to output.

Present scenario of FPOs in the country:

Presently around 5000 FPOs (including FPCs) are in existence in the country. These were formed under various initiatives of the Govt. of India (including SFAC), State Governments, NABARD, and other organisations over the last 8-10 years. (MANAGE Report, 2019). It is estimated that at best 30% of these FPCs are currently operating viably and around 20% are still struggling to survive. Around 50% are still in the mobilisation phase, equity collection, business planning other management-related developmental stages. It is quite comparable to the success rate vis-a-vis new enterprise start-ups in India's industrial and processing sector.

The FPO concept needs to be propagated and widely shared among stakeholders, and several policy-level initiatives are required to be considered:

- FPOs need to be provided seed, pesticide, insecticide, fertilizer sales license, and APMC license and dealerships on a priority basis.
- All the farmer-centric schemes of the Government may be routed through FPOs to the extent feasible.
- Reforms in the APMC Act.
- Relaxation on the extent of penalty for delayed filing of statutory documents and returns under the Companies act (Annexure 2 affixed presents changes in the proposed policy).
- Require help for infrastructure support and

technical facilities such as packhouse, warehouse, sorting and grading, packaging, material handling, transport and custom hiring equipment and machines, etc.

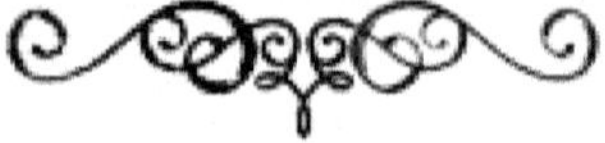

CHAPTER-13

EXPORT OPPORTUNITIES IN AGRI-PRODUCE

Export can be harnessed as a source of economic growth. As a signatory of the World Trade Organization, India has vast potential to improve its present position in the World trade of agricultural commodities both raw and processed form. The products line include cereals, pulses, oilseeds and oils, oil meal, spices and condiments, fruits and vegetables, flowers, medicinal plants and essential oils, agricultural advisory services, agricultural tools and implements, forest by-products etc.

Agricultural export is extremely important besides earning precious foreign exchange for the country; the exports help farmers/producers/exporters take advantage of a wider international market and increase their income.

Exports have also resulted in increased production in agri-sector by increasing area coverage and productivity.

As per WTO's Trade Statistics, the share of India's agricultural exports and imports in the world agriculture trade in 2017 was 2.27% and 1.90%, respectively. Even during the difficult time of pandemic lockdown, India took care not to disturb the world food supply chain and continued to export.

The agricultural exports as a percentage of India's agricultural GDP have increased from 9.4 % in 2017-18 to 9.9 % in 2018-19. While the agricultural imports as a percentage of India's agricultural GDP have declined from 5.7 % to 4.9 %, indicating exportable surplus and decreased dependence on the import of agricultural products in India.

Giant strides have been made in agri-export since independence. In 1950-51, India's Agri export was about Rs. One hundred forty-nine crores which have risen to the level of Rs. 2.53 lakh crores in 2019-20. There has been a substantial increase in export of almost all the agricultural items in the last 15 years.

However, despite being one of the top producers of agricultural products, India does not figure among the top exporters of agricultural produce.

For example, India holds the second rank in the world wheat production but ranks 34th in export. Similarly, despite being world No. 3 in the production of vegetables,

India's export ranking is the only 14th. Same is the case for fruits, where India is the second-largest producer globally, but the export ranking is 23rd.

To reach the ranks of the top exporting nation in Agriculture, and to commensurate with the production, there is a clear and categorical need to take proactive interventions.

It is also noted that Horticulture is a growing sub-sector. India holds the second position in the production of fruits and vegetables. It exports 8.23 Lakh MT (LMT) of fruits worth Rs 5,638 crore and 31.92 LMT of vegetables worth Rs 5,679 Crores annually. Grapes occupy the premier position in fresh fruit exports followed by Mango, Pomegranate, Banana, and Oranges. Onions, Mixed Vegetables, Potatoes, Tomatoes, and Green Chilly are the major items in the fresh vegetable export basket.

However, world trade of fruits and vegetables is US$ 208 billion, and India's share is minuscule. There is huge potential to increase export of fruits and vegetables. A specific strategy for export promotion has also been evolved for Fresh Fruits & Vegetables with specific emphasis on grapes, mango, pomegranate, onion, potato & Cucumber-Gherkin.

Export promotion forums (EPFs):

Export promotion forums (EPFs) for eight Agri & allied products viz. Grapes, Mango, Banana, Onion, Rice, Nutri-Cereals, Pomegranate and Floriculture, have been

constituted under the aegis of Agricultural and Processed Food Products Export Development Authority (APEDA), Department of Commerce.

They will be in touch with the producers, exporters, and other relevant stakeholders of respective commodities, hear their problems, and facilitate, support, and provide solutions.

Indian agriculture is facing two important challenges, access to affordable food for all and to ensure farmers have sufficient income to survive and thrive. Up until now, policies have largely favoured a system of subsidies and price supports. These options have become more expensive and difficult to administer, especially given commitments

India has made to trade partners elsewhere. Prospects for reform have frequently been thwarted.

Agriculture Export Policy 2018

The vision of Agriculture Export Policy is to harness the export potential of Indian agriculture, through suitable policy instruments, to make India global power in agriculture and raise farmers' income.

Objectives

- To double agricultural exports from present ~US$ 30+ Billion to ~US$ 60+ Billion by 2022 and reach US$ 100 Billion in the next few years after that, with a stable trade policy regime.
- To diversify the export basket, destinations and boost high value and value-added agricultural

exports, including a focus on perishables.

- To promote novel, indigenous, organic, ethnic, traditional and non-traditional Agri products exports.
- Enable farmers to get the benefit of export opportunities in the overseas market.
- To provide an institutional mechanism for pursuing market access, tackling barriers and deal with sanitary and phytosanitary issues.

What is the Need for the Export Policy?

- The policy can address challenges to exporting agri-products from India like low farm productivity, poor infrastructure, global price volatility to market access.

- India's share in global exports of agriculture products was merely 2.2% in 2016. India has remained at the lower end of the global agriculture export value chain given that the majority of its exports are low value, semi-processed and marketed in bulk. The share of India's high value and value-added agriculture produce in its agri-export basket is less than 15% compared to 25% in the US and 49% in China.

- India cannot export its vast horticultural produce due to lack of uniformity in quality, standardization and its inability to curtail losses across the value chain.

- Given the globalization of value chains, the country must make intensive efforts to boost high margin, value-added and branded processed products.

- The vision of doubling farmers' income by 2022 will require a series of interventions to improve production and productivity and economise the cost of production. It would also require India to augment its exports to the global market. Hence, it is necessary to have an agriculture export policy in place.

Key Recommendations of Agriculture Export Policy:

1. Stable Trade Policy Measure:

The processed agricultural products and all kinds of organic products will not be brought under the ambit of any kind of export restriction.

2. The Model Agricultural produce market committee (APMC)

All states must adopt the act, and E-NAM must be established.

3. Liberalizing Land Leasing Norms:

Contract farming is expected to bring in large-scale private investments in agriculture, thus leading to large-scale mechanization. It will further produce surplus volumes of the standardized, exportable quality of agri-products.

4. Infrastructure and Logistics Boost:

By identifying ports for the export of agri-products and development in port infrastructure like dedicated perishable

berths

5. Whole Government approach:

It will ensure all government departments and ministries like Ministry of Agriculture, Ministry of Food Processing Industries, Ministry of Shipping & Transport, Ministry of Railways and Ministry of Consumer Affairs is involved in agricultural production, processing, transportation, and export work together to address bottlenecks at every level.

6. State government involvement:

As Agriculture is a state subject, it is necessary to bring on board the state governments for positive agricultural reforms. Each state has its agricultural nuances, like one state may be experiencing drought while another may be dealing with floods. Thus it is necessary to align state agricultural policies with the nation's overarching goals.

State governments must identify the government department for the promotion of agricultural export. The states must include agriculture export in state export policy and build infrastructure and logistics to facilitate agricultural export.

7. Focus on Export centric Clusters:

Focus on export centric clusters for pre-harvest and post-harvest management of the production and upgrading the supply chain to attain much higher levels of export from those clusters

8. Promoting Value-Added Exports

Promoting value-added exports of indigenous and tribal products: Through the National Programme on Organic Production (NPOP), organic food parks, and uniform quality and packaging standards India can tap the potential for increasing organic exports. Promotion of Research & Development (R&D) activities, promoting "produce in India" through the constitution of separate funds dedicated to organic, value-added, ethnic, Geographical Indication(GI) and branded products.

9. Post-Harvest Infrastructure:

Post-harvest infrastructure can support the smooth logistical movement of agri-produce exports: This will directly correlate to increasing export volumes, assuring quality & ensuring better price realization per unit.

10. Digitization of land records:

Digitalization of land records, geo-mapping of lands, registration of farmers and farm producer organizations (FPOs) is critical to smooth agricultural exports.

11. Establishment of Strong Quality Regime:

With the focus on strong R&D, new varieties, state of the art lab and a lab networking process for effective accreditation and monitoring will be established. An institutional mechanism should be provided that would pursue market access, tackle barriers and deal with sanitary and phytosanitary (inspection of plant disease in agri-produce) issues against India's agricultural exports that come up from time to time.

12. Research and Development (R&D):

R&D led by private industry and higher infrastructure spending by the government will be the key to boosting agricultural exports. Along with this, innovations in packaging, improving the shelf life of products and greater R&D in developing products to suit importing countries' palates should be a priority. The policy has recommended setting up an agri-startup fund.

India and the World Trade Organization:

India has been a member of General Agreement on Tariffs and Trade (GATT) since 8 July 1948 and a World Trade Organisation (WTO) member since 1 January 1995. In an interplay of trade and commerce in a global village, WTO may be the referee. It was created for the liberalization of international trade. WTO deals with the rules of trade and implementing new trade agreements

India is one of the founding members of WTO along with more than 130 other countries. Various trade disputes of

India with other nations have been settled through WTO. By being a WTO member, several countries are now trading with India, thus giving a boost to production, employment, the standard of living and an opportunity to maximize the use of the world resources.

Significantly, the BRICS group (Brazil, India, China and South Africa) is increasingly recognized as pivotal in

furthering International Trade progress. The Group of 33 developing countries, including India and China, has proposed to include procurement of food products from farmers at minimum support price (MSP) and their distribution at subsidised rates to poor. Subsidies on account of these programmes should not be included in the category of trade-distorting subsidies that disrupt markets and prices of food items. These special and differential provisions balance out the commercial interests of the developed countries and are essential to protect the livelihood interests of the small and marginal farmers in the developing world for whom agriculture is not an issue of trade but of livelihood and existence.

Overview

Tackling these challenges requires a comprehensive, multi-faceted approach that includes spurring investments into India's infrastructure and opening foreign market access for India's goods and services. Besides, plugging India into Asia's production value chains is a crucial pathway to taking full advantage of an established service.

Reforms in the sector by investing in new agricultural technologies, research and development, technical training, and developing quality and efficient food management have become essential.

India's firm view is: "The world is not static nor is the challenges and issues that affect global trade."

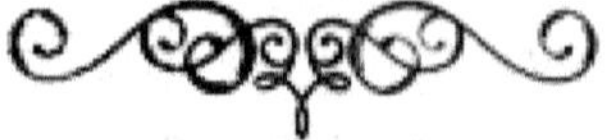

CHAPTER-14

FOOD SECURITY FOR ALL
(A global challenge)

"Food security exists when all people, at all times, have physical and economic access to sufficient, safe and nutritious food that meets their dietary needs and food preferences for an active and healthy life."

(Definition agreed to at the 1996 World Food Summit)

The right to food

The right to adequate food is a universal human right that is realized when all people have physical and economic access at all times to adequate food or the means for its procurement, without discrimination of any kind. The world can produce enough food to feed everyone adequately. Despite progress made over the past two decades, about 793 million (2015) people in the world, or just over one in every nine human beings, still suffer from hunger daily. While it had decreased from 18.6 per cent in 1990-92 to less than 11 per cent in 2014-16, this persistently high number remains unacceptable. Beyond its ethical dimension, hunger and food insecurity takes an enormous toll on economies and have adverse consequences for vulnerable populations' livelihoods and economic capabilities. The costs to society are enormous in terms of lost productivity, health, well-being, decreased learning ability, and reduced human potential fulfilment.

Food Security for future generation:

Global challenges will require global cooperation. In facing megatrends such as a population boom in a hyper-urbanized world, countries cannot afford to leave corners of the world with unexploited agricultural potentials. Increased investment and technology transfers are sorely needed. With climate change disrupting entire supply chains and generating waves of climate and food refugees, it is clear no country will be able to claim to be food secure without regional and international cooperation.

Developed Countries:

In Europe, the United States, and other high-income regions and countries, consumers have become complacent about the food system's ability to deliver the food they want and need. The use of "improved."

Technologies, incorporating scientific knowledge and significant capital investment, has enabled producers to generate substantial volumes of food per unit of natural resource input at affordable prices.

New storage technologies have reduced losses and, combined with transport improvements, have limited supply disruptions. Processing technologies have multiplied the number of consumable products derived from a particular crop or animal.

Wholesale and retail sales operations have become increasingly efficient in providing the final link to the consumer. Together, production, storage, processing, and delivery operations combine in variable ways and form robust, demand-driven agricultural value chains that deliver safe and tasty food, on a reliable basis, to many consumers.

Competition among participants in all segments of the chains helps to ensure that costs are controlled, and products are affordable to even low-income consumers in those regions and countries.

Developing Countries:

By contrast, in many parts of the developing world, much of agriculture is based upon traditional technologies. Yields remain low; storage is rudimentary and inadequate to prevent major losses.

Modern food systems are more successful in producing

reliable food supplies, but even wealthy, surplus-producing countries do not assure that food is available cheaply enough for all consumers. Supplementary public assistance, such as Public Distribution System (PDS), food stamps etc. is necessary to cover the affordability

It is generally agreed that in the next decades, growing populations and economic expansion will inevitably create supply disruptions. It will put upward pressure on prices unless agricultural production and productivity are increased; trade mechanisms become much more efficient, and policies are changed. Greater productivity in temperate zones could partially compensate for this decline.

What needs to be done?

Our food systems do not operate in isolation. They are part of an environment, and the road ahead is paved with hurdles. If anything is evident, meeting future food demand will require a complete reinvention of our global food system away from the current status quo.

This will mean rethinking and restructuring everything from the technologies we use, the scale of investments in the agriculture and food sectors, and our welfare programs and diets. We will need to produce more and better. While no country or city start at the same point, all need to adapt. No one solution fits all from net exporters to importers and urbanized Singapore to highly deserted Saudi Arabia.

While current and future challenges differ from those of the past, responses to the new challenges can build on lessons learned.

Experience tells us that there is an urgent need for a universal agenda, country and context-specific strategies, and people-centred approaches. Appropriate governance mechanisms need to be established at regional and country levels.

At the global level, the Committee on World Food Security (CFS) provides a unique food security governance platform. Good practices that lead to greater impact, including human rights-based approaches and gender-sensitive policies, programmes and investments, need to be promoted.

Accountability mechanisms and monitoring capacities need to be strengthened in national policies, programmes and investments, to ensure the greatest possible impact.

According to the Food and Agriculture Organization of the United Nations (FAO), over 70 per cent of the world's food needs are met by small farmers. Agriculture is the economic sector that employs the most people in the world and the main source of food and income for many people living in poverty. Thus, investing in agriculture is not only one of the most effective strategies to improve food security and promote sustainability; it is also essential to many countries' economic development. Policies designed to promote agribusiness and sustainable food value chains play a crucial role in achieving food security for all.

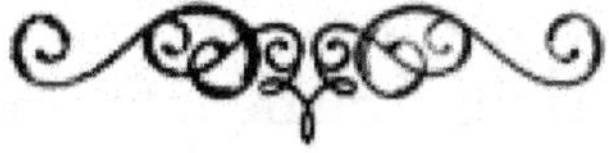

CHAPTER-15

SUSTAINABLE AGRICULTURE

Sustainable agricultural development means: *"Obtaining optimal production without damaging natural resources."*

It ensures the efficient production of high-quality agricultural products, protects the natural environment, improves farmers' social and economic conditions, and safeguards the ecosystem.

Major challenges-

Persistently high levels of hunger and unsustainable human activity present a major challenge for agriculture. To meet the growing food-demand of over nine billion people, by 2050, agriculture will need to produce 50% more food globally in the same period. Moreover, One-third

of farmland is degraded, up to 75 % of crop genetic diversity has been lost, and 13 million hectares of forests a year is converted into other land uses.

Competition over natural resources is continuously intensifying. It is coming from urban expansion, expansion of agriculture at the expense of forests, industrial use of water, and recreational use of land.

Climate change is also reducing the resilience of production systems and leading to natural resource degradation. Temperature-increase, modified rainfall areas and extreme weather conditions are expected to become significantly more severe in the future;

The increasing mobility of people and goods, environmental changes, and changes in production practices have given rise to new threats from diseases or invasive species, affecting food safety, human health and sustainability of production systems. Inadequate policies and technical capacities compound threats. The policy agenda and mechanisms for production and resource conservation are mostly disjointed.

To be sustainable, agriculture must meet the needs of present and future generations for its products and services, while ensuring profitability, environmental health and social and economic equity.

Steps towards archiving goals through sustainability-

The challenges of increasing food production are daunting. Future production-increase depends mainly on increasing the productivity of existing agricultural land and water resources. Farmer involvement is the key to sustainable agriculture. Given the right incentives and government support, farm families can make significant progress towards managing their land and water sustainably.

In both developed and developing countries, Agricultural Systems need to use new approaches to increase food supplies. Strategic development of new approaches and the transition to sustainability is needed.

Improving efficiency in the use of natural resources is crucial to sustainable agriculture. Direct action to be taken to conserve, protect and enhance natural resources .e.g. Agroforestry development.

A diversity of crops and crop rotation can help plants fix their own nitrogen and balance pests and predators. It recycles the soil's nutrients and reduces the reliance on inputs such as mineral fertilizers and chemical pesticides.

By diversifying farming systems, making greater use of the plant's biological and genetic potential, improving the management of natural resources, and developing agroforestry systems can help maintain soil fertility.

Good governance is essential for the sustainability of both the natural and human systems. Policies and institutions are needed for the adoption and regulation of sustainable practices.

Sustainable agricultural practices must make full use of technology, research and development, though with much greater local knowledge integration than in the past. It will require new and more robust partnerships between technical and investment-oriented organizations.
They are using the modern farm management technology so that the natural resource base is not altered and sustained for future use by coming generations, e.g. Resource Conservation technologies, like Zero tillage, technologies to conserve water and energy etc.
The ultimate objective should be the optimum mix of agricultural practices, both old and new, in order to maximize sustainable output within the limits of available resources

Overview

Sustainable agriculture must nurture healthy ecosystems and support the sustainable management of land, water and natural resources while ensuring world food security. To be sustainable, agriculture must meet the needs of present and future generations for its products and services, while ensuring profitability, environmental health and social and economic equity.

CHAPTER-16

INCREASING FARMERS' INCOME
(DFI Report)

Farmers' income can be increased if technology, input prices, wages and labour use could result in per-unit cost saving. Then the farmer's income would increase at a much higher rate than the output. Another source is the relative increase in prices of farm products compared to the prices of non-agricultural commodities.

The Government constituted an Inter-ministerial Committee in April 2016 to examine issues relating to "Doubling of Farmers Income" (DFI) and recommend strategies to achieve the same. The Committee submitted its Report to the Government in September 2018 containing the strategy for doubling farmers' income by 2022.

The DFI strategy, as recommended by the Committee, includes seven sources of income growth:

- improvement in crop productivity
- Improvement in livestock productivity.
- Resource use efficiency or saving in cost of production.
- Increase in cropping intensity.

- Diversification towards high-value crops.
- Improvement in real prices received by farmers
- Shift from farm to non-farm occupations.

The DFI Committee addresses agriculture as a value-led enterprise. It suggests empowering farmers with "improved market linkages" and enabling "self-sustainable models" as the basis for continued productivity-production and income growth for farmers.

It builds the basic strategic direction for five primary concerns:

- Optimal monetisation of farmers' produce,
- Sustainability of production,
- Improved resource use efficiency,
- Re-strengthening of extension and knowledge-based services, and
- Risk management.

The DFI Committee deliberates upon specific economic activities and topics that have a durable impact on farmers' income.

Some of these are categorised as follows:

- Demand-Driven Agricultural Logistics System for post-production operations such as produce aggregation, transportation, warehousing, etc

- Developing Hub and Spoke System at the back-end and front-end to facilitate and promote a new market architecture so that all kinds of farmers can avail services that empower them to physically connect and supply to any market in the country of their choice.

- Marketing Intelligence System to provide a demand-led decision-making support system, forecasting system for agricultural produce demand and supply, and crop area estimation to aid price stabilisation and risk management.

- Agricultural Value System (AVS) as an integration of the supply chain and to drive market-led value system – District level, State level and National Level Value-System Platforms to promote individual value chains to integrate into a sector-wide supply chain

- Farmer-centric National Agricultural Marketing System: by restructuring for a new market architecture, consisting of Primary Retail Agriculture Markets (PRAMs/GrAMs are numbering 22,000) and Primary Wholesale Agricultural Markets (APMCs/APLMs-other markets numbering around 10,000), as also secondary & tertiary agricultural markets, all of which are networked by online platforms to facilitate pan-India market access; as also integrating the domestic market with the export market by considering the latter as targeted market activity and not just an add-on.

- Promotion of Sustainable-Agriculture: Climate Resilient Agriculture, Rainfed Agriculture, Conservation Agriculture, Ecology Farming, Watershed Management System, Integrated Farming System, Organic Farming, Agro-Climatic Regional Planning, Agricultural Resources Management and Micro-Level Planning, etc.

While the above alternate systems are to be adopted & scaled up, the modern agrochemical based cultivation practices shall be promoted.

- Effective Input Management achieving Resource-Use-Efficiency (RUE) and Total Factor Productivity (TFP) – Water, soil, fertilisers, seeds, labour-farm mechanisation, credit and precision farming, to reduce farm losses, while ensuring sustainable and eco-friendly practices
- Enhancing Production through Productivity: to achieve & sustain higher production out of less and release land and water resources to diversify into higher-value farming for enhanced income.
- Farm Linked Activities: to include secondary agriculture that utilises local workforce and biological resource in farms' vicinity. These comprise manufacturing and services activities of KVIC (Khadi and Village Industries Commission) and MSME (Micro, Small and Medium Enterprises) scale, for promoting near-farm and off-farm income-generating opportunities as well as to facilitate more of the farm produce to capture more of the market value.

- Agricultural Risk Assessment and Management including drought management, demand &

price forecast, weather forecast, management of biotic stress including vertebrate pests, access to credit

among farmers for farming operations; providing long term credit, post-production finance to preventing distress sale by farmers, and crop & animal risk management through insurance.

- Empowering Farmers through Agricultural Extension, Knowledge Diffusion and Skill Development are also ensured.

- Research & Development and ICT designed to support the Doubling of Farmers' Income strategy in the short run, and help accelerate the pace of income enhancement on a sustainable basis in the long run.

- Structural and Governance Reforms in Agriculture, including building a database of farmers, facilitating farmer & produce mobilisation, an institutional mechanism at district, state & national levels for coordination & convergence, digital monitoring dashboard at district, state & national level for seamless & real-time monitoring of field delivery, utilising Panchayat Raj Institutions, and farm income measurement as key delivery channels for transparent and inclusive development.

Various interventions and schemes launched for the benefit of farmers:

- To provide income support to all farmers, to enable them to take care of expenses related to agriculture and allied activities and domestic needs, PM-KISAN provides a payment of Rs. 6000/- per year.

- To provide a social security net for Small and Marginal Farmers (SMF) Pradhan Mantri Kisan MaanDhan Yojana (PM-KMY) for providing old-age pension to these farmers   Rs. 3000/- on attaining the age of 60 years.
- To provide better insurance coverage to crops for risk mitigation, Pradhan Mantri Fasal Bima Yojana (PMFBY) provides insurance cover for all stages of the crop cycle including post-harvest risks in specified instances, with a low premium contribution by farmers.
- Minimum Support Price (MSPs)is increased for all Kharif & Rabi crops for 2018-19 season at a level of at least 150 per cent of the cost of production
- Distribution of Soil Health Cards to farmers to rationalize the use of fertilizers
- "Per drop more crop" initiative under which drip/sprinkler irrigation is being encouraged for optimal water utilisation, reducing the cost of inputs and increasing productivity.
- "Paramparagat Krishi Vikas Yojana (PKVY)" for promoting organic farming
- Launch of the e-NAM initiative to provide farmers with an electronic transparent and competitive online trading platform.
- Under "Har Medh Par Ped", agroforestry is being promoted for additional income.
- PM-Annadata Aay Sanrakshan Abhiyan scheme aims to ensure remunerative prices to the farm-

ers for their produce to protect the farmers' income which is expected to go a long way towards the welfare of farmers.

- The flow of adequate credit to the agriculture sector, by providing interest subvention of 2% on short-term crop loans up to Rs.3.00 lakh

Various Reforms and amendments executed:

- Model APLMC (Promotion & Facilitation) Act, 2017
- Establishment of 22,000 number of Gramin Agriculture Markets (GrAMs) as aggregation platforms
- Agri-Export Policy that targets to double agri-exports by 2022
- The Farmers Produce Trade and Commerce (Promotion & Facilitation) Act, 2020
- The Farmers (Empowerment & Protection) Agreement on Price Assurance and Farm Services Act, 2020
- Amendments to the Essential Commodities Act, 1955, that deregulates various agri-commodities
- Promotion of 10,000 FPOs by 2024

Creation of Corpus Funds:

- Micro Irrigation Fund – Rs. 5,000 crore
- Agri-marketing Fund to strengthen eNAM and GrAMs – Rs. 2,000 crore
- Agricultural Infrastructure Fund (AIF) to build agri-logistics (backward & forward linkages) – Rs. 1 lakh crore

Overview

The DFI Report's underlying theme is to promote agriculture as an enterprise and farmer as an entrepreneur necessitating the adoption of business principles for positive net returns. Further, the agriculture sector as a profession will become wholesome when the transition happens from, food security to nutrition security. It will be for the consumers, extractive production system to a sustainable production system for the ecology, and a mere Green Revolution to move towards a Farmers' Income Revolution or Income Revolution for the farmers.

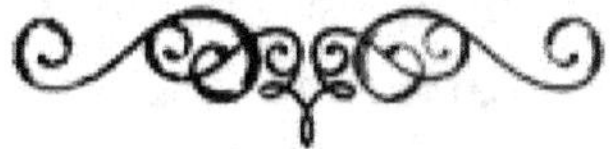

CHAPTER-17

HARYANA: BREAD BASKET OF INDIA

Haryana has been at the forefront in adopting the latest technologies in agri-business. It is also counted as one of the leading states for Agriculture production in the country. Haryana hosts about 2% of India's population. With an area of 44.21 lakh hectare state occupies approximately 1.37% of the total geographical area. Barely three decades into existence has Haryana created a distinct place for itself. As the largest recipient of investment per capita since 2000 in India, and among one of the wealthiest and most economically developed regions in South Asia, Haryana has India's third-highest per capita income at ₹214,509   against the national average of ₹112,432 in the year 2016–17. Haryana is self-sufficient in food production and the second largest contributor to India's central pool of food grains. The state makes an incredible contribution of 14 per cent to the Central Pool.

The major Kharif crops are rice, jawar, bajra, maize, cotton, jute, sugarcane, sesame and groundnut, sown in April and May and harvested in November. The major Rabi crops are wheat, tobacco, gram, linseed, rapeseed and mustard, sown in late October or early November and harvested in

March. About 86% of the area is arable, and of that 96% is cultivated. About 75% of the area is irrigated, through tube wells and an extensive system of canals. About 2/3rd of the State has assured irrigation, most suited for a rice-wheat production system. In contrast, rain-fed lands (around 1/5th) are most suited for rapeseed & mustard, pearl millet, cluster bean cultivation, agro-forestry and arid-horticulture.

The state bordering National Capital Region (NCR) ideal location enables access to a range of big markets and the international airport. Rice, wheat, rapeseed & mustard, bajra, cotton and sugarcane are the major crops with considerable scope for agricultural diversification as well as off farm opportunities. Cauliflower, onion, potato, tomato, chillies, guava, and kinnow are important horti-cultural crops with good potential. Allied sectors like dairying, poultry, fishery, arid- horticulture, mushroom farming, beekeeping, and agro-forestry have great poten-tial. 37 mandis in the State have been connected with the e-NAM (National Agricultural Market) scheme to make the system for marketing of agricultural produce smooth and transparent . However, the share of agriculture sector in the state's economy has been declining over the years. Haryana is among the top ten producers of food grains.

Haryana ranks 22nd in fruit production, ranks 11th in vege-table production, and 11th in total fertilizer consump-tion.

Soil-profile of Haryana -

Soil constitutes the most precious natural resource of the state. Many soils are found in Haryana due to the marked variations in the physiographic and climatic conditions.

The soil in Haryana is formed entirely of alluvium. The state is situated towards the depression of the rivers Ganges and Indus. It has a broad level plain moist land standing on the watershed between the basin of

The soil profile reflects that major parts of Panipat, Sonipat, Palwal, Northeastern part of Jhajjar, and Faridabad districts fall under the medium-fertility zone. While, the eastern part of Panipat, Sonipat, Faridabad and Palwal lie under low to medium fertility zone. District Rohtak, Jhajjar and central upper part of Gurgaon lie in low fertility zone. The rest of the areas are under poor fertility zones especially of Rewari, Mewat southern part of Gurgaon and western part of Palwal and Faridabad.

Scope of agribusiness in Haryana –

There is a continuous growth in agricultural inputs like high variety seeds, inorganic fertilizers and bio-pesticides. Bio-technology applications in the production of seeds, manure, biofuel from paralli (stalks), organic pesticides, microbes for bakery industry etc. is gaining popularity.

There are two ways to increase production: expand the area under production that grows food or intensify production per unit area of land (or both). Those places where nearly maximum yields achieved sill can improve productivity by 25–50 per cent. In poor fertility areas, suitable agroforestry which needed less water and nutrients can be promoted. Those under the medium-fertility area can be improved by adding organic fertilizers and new species or verities can be grown under controlled conditions in poly-houses.

New storage warehouses and cold storage chains are being

established, and agro-cluster is specified to promote pro-cessing and value addition to agri-produce at local levels to contribute to exports. Mega food Parks, Cold storage chains, Processing units, Ethanol-Plants are being estab-lished. Digitization of land records, Farmers Portal, Direct transfer of subsidies to the farmer, registration of crops on portal etc. is helping the farmers to get help in one click. Steps are being taken to improve co-operatives' working and registration of new organisations and companies in agro-business to promote processing, storage, and export.

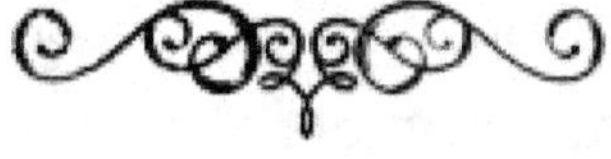

CHAPTER-18

SCOPE FOR AGRIBUSINESS IN INDIA

India is endowed with varied agro-climate, which facilitates temperate, sub-tropical and tropical agricultural commodities. There is a growing demand for agricultural inputs like feed and fodder, inorganic fertilizers, bio-fertilizers. Biotechnology applications in agriculture have vast scope in production of seed, bio-control agents, and microbes' industrial harnessing for bakery products. Export can be harnessed as a source of economic growth. As a signatory of the World Trade Organization, India has vast potential to improve its present position in the World trade of agricultural commodities both raw and processed form.

Pradhan Mantri Kisan SAMPADA Yojana:

Government of India (GOI) has approved a new Central Sector Scheme – Pradhan Mantri Kisan SAMPADA
Yojana. This comprehensive package will create modern infrastructure with efficient supply chain management from farm gate to retail outlet. It will provide a big boost to the growth of the food processing sector in the country and provide better returns to farmers, creating huge employment opportunities in rural areas, reducing wastage of agricultural produce, increasing the processing level, and enhancing the export of the processed foods.

Mega Food Park:

The Scheme of Mega Food Park aims to provide a mechanism to link agricultural production to the market by bringing together farmers, processors, and retailers to ensure maximizing value addition, minimizing wastage, increasing farmers' income, and creating employment opportunities particularly in the rural sector.

The Mega Food Park Scheme is based on the "Cluster" approach. It envisages creating the state of the art support infrastructure in a well-defined Agri / horticultural zone for setting up modern food processing units in the industrial plots provided in the park with the well-established supply chain. Mega food park typically consists of supply chain infrastructure including collection centres, primary processing centres, central processing centres, cold chain and around 25-30 fully developed plots for entrepreneurs to set up food processing units.

So far, 22 Mega Food Parks are operational. The Mega Food Park project is implemented by a Special Purpose Vehicle (SPV), a Body Corporate registered under the Companies Act.
Cold Chain:

The objective of the Cold Chain scheme is Value Addition and Preservation Infrastructure. It provides integrated cold chain and preservation infrastructure facilities, without any break, from the farm gate to the consumer.

It covers the creation of an infrastructure facility. It includes the entire supply chain viz. pre-cooling, weighing, sorting, grading, waxing facilities at the farm level. It also embraces multi-product/ multi-temperature cold storage, CA storage, packing facility, IQF, blast freezing in the distribution hub. Reefer vans and mobile cooling units help to facilitate the distribution of organic produce, marine, dairy, meat and poultry etc.

The scheme allows flexibility in project planning, emphasising the creation of cold chain infrastructure at the farm level. The integrated cold chain project is set up by Partnership / Proprietorship Firms, Companies, Corporations, Cooperatives, Self Help Groups (SHGs), Farmer Producer Organizations (FPOs), NGOs, Central / State PSUs, etc.

Creation/ Expansion of Food Processing/ Preservation Capacities (Unit Scheme):

The main objective of the Scheme is the creation of processing and preservation capacities, and modernisation/ expansion of existing food processing units to increase the level of processing, value addition leading to reduction of wastage. The processing activities undertaken by the individual unit covers a wide range of post-harvest processes resulting in value addition and/or enhancing shelf life with specialized facilities required for the preservation of perishables.

While the expansion of processing capacity is necessary to increase the level of processing and reduce wastage, the induction of modern technology is intended to make a clear difference in process efficiencies and improve the quality of the end product. The setting up of new units and modernization/expansion of existing units are covered under the scheme.

Scheme is implemented through organizations such as Central & State PSUs/ Joint Ventures/ Farmer Producers

Organization (FPOs)/ NGOs/ Cooperatives/ SHG's/ Pvt. Ltd companies/ individuals proprietorship firms engaged in establishment/ up-gradation/ modernization of food processing units.

Agro Processing Cluster:

The scheme aims to develop modern infrastructure and common facilities to encourage a group of entrepreneurs to set up food processing units based on cluster approach by linking groups of producers/ farmers to the processors and markets through the well-equipped supply chain with modern infrastructure.

Each agro-processing clusters under the scheme have two basic components, i.e. Basic Enabling Infrastructure (roads, water supply, power supply, drainage, ETP etc.), Core Infrastructure/ Common facilities (warehouses, cold storages, IQF, tetra pack, sorting, grading etc.) and at least five food processing units with a minimum investment of Rs. 25 crores.

Scheme for Creation of Backward and Forward Linkages:

The scheme's objective is to provide effective and seamless backward and forward integration for the processed food industry by plugging the gaps in the supply chain in terms of availability of raw material and linkages with the market. Under the scheme, financial assistance is provided for setting up primary processing centres/ collection centres at farm gate and modern retail outlets at the front end and connectivity through insulated/ refrigerated transport.

Food Safety & Quality Assurance Infrastructure:

Quality and Food Safety have become a competitive edge in the global market for food products. For the country's food processing sector's all-around development, various aspects of Total Quality Management (TQM) such as quality control, quality system, and quality assurance should operate horizontally. Apart from this, in the interest of consumer safety and public health, there is a need to ensure that the quality food products manufactured and sold in the market meet the food safety regulator's stringent parameters.

Keeping in view the objectives above, the government has been extending financial assistance under the scheme under the following components:
The Scheme applies to perishable horticulture and non-horticulture produce such as fruits, vegetables, dairy products, meat, poultry, fish, Ready to Cook Food Products, Honey, Coconut, Spices, Mushroom, Retails Shops for Perishable Food Products etc. The Scheme would enable linking farmers to processors and the market to ensure remunerative prices for Agri produce.
Skill Development:

The Ministry of Food Processing Industries is working in close collaboration with other related agencies to augment skilled human resources in the food processing sector through the National Institute of Food Technology Entrepreneurship and Management (NIFTEM). It will address the skill gap in the food processing sector and to provide sector-specific skilled workforce from floor level workers, operators, packaging and assembly line workers to quality control supervisor etc. in the various segments of food processing industries,

At present processing is done at the primary level only and the rising standard of living expands opportunities for secondary and tertiary processing of agricultural commodities.

Mushroom production for domestic consumption and export can be enhanced with improvement in the state of the art of their production.

Organic farming has the highest potential in India as the pesticide and inorganic fertilizer application are less in India than in industrial nations of the world. The farmers can be encouraged and educated to switch over to organic farming.

There is wide scope for production and promotion of bio-pesticides and bio-control agents for the protection of crops.

Micro-irrigation systems and labour-saving farm equipment have good potential for years to come due to declining groundwater level and labour scarcity for agricultural operations like weeding, transplanting and harvesting.

Seeds, hybrid and genetically modified crops, have the highest potential in India in the future.

Production of vegetables and flowers under greenhouse conditions can be taken up to harness the export market. The forest resources can be utilized for the production of by-products of forestry.

Beekeeping and apiary can be taken up on a large scale in India.

Trained human resources in agriculture and allied sciences
will take on agricultural extension systems due to dwindling state finance resources and downsizing the present government agricultural extension staff as consulting ser-

vices.

The enhanced agricultural production throws open employment opportunities in marketing, transport, cold storage and warehousing facilities, credit, insurance and logistic support services.

Types of Small Agro-businesses:

The small Agro-businesses can be classified as the following types

- Production: It includes all types of agricultural production of crops and forestry.
- Distribution: It refers to those businesses that do not make anything but bring the goods and services to the consumer. It includes packaging, labelling, transporting, refrigerating, freezing, processing, storing, and performing any service necessary to prepare the goods or provide the service to the eventual consumer.
- Retailing: Although often included as a phase of distribution, retailing is listed as a separate category because many persons are employed in retailing. It represents one of the best opportunities for the potential entrepreneur. Retailing is that stage of distribution, which deals with the consumers. Examples of retailers are grocers, agricultural input retailing, vendors etc.
- Personal services: The service business is those, which do

not primarily supply goods to the public, but instead perform a service. Examples of personal service are insurance agents, agro-service centres.

- Financial: Financial businesses are usually service-oriented, but they deal primarily with the loaning or investing of money. Examples of financial services are commercial banks, insurance companies, and loan societies etc.

- Franchising: Franchising is a system for selectively distributing goods or services through outlets owned by the franchisee. According to prearranged terms and conditions, it is a patent or trademark, license, entitling the holder to market particular products or services under a brand name or trademark.

The franchiser is the owner of his or her own business. Examples-Organic Food Franchise, Outdoor Farm Equipment Franchise, e.g. Agrimart, one of the biggest players in the supply of outdoor farm equipment is heading towards becoming a leader in providing farm equipment like irrigation machinery, pipes etc. and is operating pan India, Vegetable and Fruits' Franchise, e.g. Organo Best provides high-quality vegetables and fruits)

Small agro-business and entrepreneur a propellant of the economy:

An individual entrepreneur is a person who innovates, allocates and manages the factors of production and bears the risk. She/he can perceive latent economic opportunities and devise their exploitation; an entrepreneur conceives
the ideas of business, design the organization of firms, accumulates capital, recruits labour, establishes relations with supplier, customers, and the government converts the conception into a functional organization.

An Individual entrepreneur is the supplier of resources,

supervisor and coordinator and ultimate decision-maker.

Entrepreneurs are the human agent in economic development as they combine talents, abilities and drive to transform resources into profitable undertakings. The economy is propelled by the activities of persons who wanted to promote new goods and new methods of productions or exploit a new source of materials or new market not merely for profit but also for creating.

Entrepreneurs are looking out for new ideas and willing to take the risk of introducing them. It is an interesting process involving the economic, social and political sectors of society, including the emergence of corps of entrepreneurs who are psychologically motivated and technologically prepared regularly to lead the way in introducing new production functions in the economy's growth.
Entrepreneurial opportunities in Modern Agriculture:

One of the most important assets of any business owner is a personality, which lends itself to the type of business chosen. There are many different kinds of business and innumerable types of personalities.

Therefore, an objective self-examination is necessary for the discovery of personal strengths and weaknesses, especially as they relate to owning a particular type of business.

Few qualities to inculcate: Vision, Knowledge of business, Creativeness, Initiative, Ability to work with others, Self-confidence, Adaptability, Enthusiasm, Ability to organize, make decisions, take responsibility, accept suggestions

Micro, Small, and Medium Enterprises (MSME)

MSME stands for Micro, Small, and Medium Enterprises under the Micro, Small, and Medium Enterprises Development (MSMED) Act in 2006.MSMEs have created 11 crore job opportunities in India while contributing to the GDP by 29%. It enables Indian enterprises to carry out their businesses better. It also works hand-in-hand towards the development of the nation's backward and rural areas.

'Atma Nirbhar Bharat Abhiyan' or the Self-Reliant India Scheme of 2020 by the Government of India has given a new definition for MSMEs-

(i) A micro enterprise, where the investment in Plant and Machinery or Equipment does not exceed one crore rupees and turnover does not exceed five crore rupees;

(ii) A small enterprise, where the investment in Plant and Machinery or Equipment does not exceed ten crore rupees and turnover does not exceed fifty crore rupees;

(iii) A medium enterprise, where the investment in Plant and Machinery or Equipment does not exceed fifty crore rupees and turnover does not exceed two hundred and fifty crore rupees.

Objectives of a Small Business:

Service, Profit, Community participation, Growth and Subsidiaries are the objectives towards which all the organisation's activities are directed. Small business and small-scale units are characterized by smallness, involves lesser capital and mostly one-man venture. They are highly diversified – a wide range of products, Wide dispersal geographically,

Importance to our economy:

They are important sources of competition and challenge the economic power of larger firms. They broaden the distribution of economic and political power and do not result in the concentration of power. They are the sources of innovation and creativity. They offer career opportunities to those who are the most productive in a small company's unstructured environment, Provide the dynamism, innovation, and effectiveness that lead to the productive economic system. There exist vast agri-business opportunities in developing economy of India.

Advantages and Disadvantages of small business:

Advantages: less capital outlay, but more employment the generation does not require sophisticated technology, facilitates decentralization and dispersal of business units, offers a wide range of choices to consumers, can serve specialized needs and utilizes the resources in full without wastage. Disadvantages are inadequate management ability, inadequate finance, Poor competitive position and uncertain business continuity.

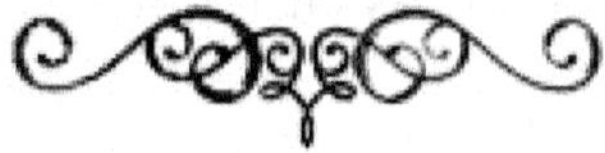

IN THE END

At the onset of the COVID-19 pandemic, in Mid-March of 2020, online grocery stores showed a boom in their sales. There were nearly 200 items available with them at least 120 local items. Local farmers filled well over thousands of orders. This joint venture of farmers and general stores helped sell a large chunk of fruits and vegetable produce to restaurants, school, hospitals and homes. The pandemic paved the way to transport and deliver the farm produce direct-to-consumer. These opportunities ultimately opened the floodgates for many farm-businesses to flourish. This is a time when the world has accelerated its efforts and actions to control climate change and food security. Sustainable development cannot be delayed anymore. If human civilization has to continue on this earth, then it is must to use the technology for preservation and advancement of our natural resources. Agribusiness has brought such opportunities and challenges before the world.

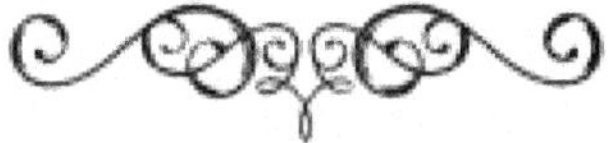